LATINO BIOGRAPHY LIBRARY

Sandra Cisneros

Inspiring Latina Author

KAREN CLEMENS WARRICK

Enslow Publishers, Inc.
40 Industrial Road
Box 398
Berkeley Heights, NJ 07922
USA

http://www.enslow.com

Library of Congress Cataloging-in-Publication Data

Warrick, Karen Clemens.
    Sandra Cisneros : inspiring Latina author / Karen Clemens Warrick.
        p. cm. — (Latino biography library)
    Includes bibliographical references (p.   ) and index.
    Summary: "Discusses the life of Latina author Sandra Cisneros, including her childhood in Chicago, her path to becoming an accomplished author, and her work in the Latino community"—Provided by publisher.
    ISBN-13: 978-0-7660-3162-3
    ISBN-10: 0-7660-3162-4
    1. Cisneros, Sandra—Juvenile literature. 2. Authors, American—20th century—Biography—Juvenile literature. 3. Mexican American authors—Biography—Juvenile literature. 4. Mexican American women—Biography—Juvenile literature. I. Title.
    PS3553.I78Z95 2009
    813'.54—dc22
    [B]
                                                                            2008041798

Printed in the United States of America

10 9 8 7 6 5 4 3 2 1

To Our Readers: We have done our best to make sure all Internet Addresses in this book were active and appropriate when we went to press. However, the author and the publisher have no control over and assume no liability for the material available on those Internet sites or on other Web sites they may link to. Any comments or suggestions can be sent by e-mail to comments@enslow.com or to the address on the back cover.

♻ Enslow Publishers, Inc., is committed to printing our books on recycled paper. The paper in every book contains 10% to 30% post-consumer waste (PCW). The cover board on the outside of each book contains 100% PCW. Our goal is to do our part to help young people and the environment too!

Illustration Credits: Associated Press, pp. 39, 48, 69, 78, 97; Carol M. Highsmith/Everett Collection, p. 58; Courtesy of Carolyn S. Shealer, pp. 28, 32, 33; Getty Images, p. 1; Hillery Smith/MCT/Landov, p. 87; Jason Koski, Cornell University Photography, p. 101; June Hymas, p. 46; Keith Levit/Shutterstock, p. 45; Mary Evans Picture Library/Everett Collection, pp. 23, 31; Michael E. Casey, pp. 74, 82; Milbert O. Brown/MCT/Landov, pp. 7, 16; Sharon M. Steinman/MCT/Landov, pp. 3, 4.

Cover Illustration: Sandra Cisneros in a brown shawl. Getty Images.

Contents

Sandra Cisneros has much to smile about as one of the world's most successful Mexican-American authors.

The House
on Mango Street

In 1976, twenty-two-year-old Sandra Cisneros was living away from home for the first time. She had moved to Iowa to study creative writing.

Iowa City was different from Cisneros's hometown. In Iowa, most families lived in houses with yards. They came from similar backgrounds. Cisneros had grown up in Chicago, Illinois. Her home there was an apartment building. Lots of people from many different cultures lived in her neighborhood.

Cisneros was not like other students in her classes at the University of Iowa. Her childhood experiences were different from theirs. She did not fit in and felt like an outsider. For the first time, she said she was "ashamed when she spoke in class, so she chose not to speak."[1]

One of her professors assigned a book that talked about the house of imagination. It compared storage places for memories to areas in a house. Memories were stored in the attic, stairways, and the cellars. This puzzled Cisneros. Her concept of a house was a one-floor apartment. Her family's apartment did not have an attic. The stairwells were public places used by everyone. Spiders and mice lived in the basement. No one wanted to store things down there. The book said the house of imagination was a familiar, comforting place. It was not familiar to Cisneros. She could not picture a "house" like that one.[2]

As other students talked about the attics, stairways, and cellars of childhood memories, Cisneros felt more out of place. Everyone else seemed to share the same knowledge. Cisneros felt "homeless. There were no attics and cellars and crannies. I had no such house in my memories," she said. "This caused me to question myself. . . . What did I know? What could I know? My classmates were from the best schools in the country. They had been bred as fine hothouse flowers. I was a yellow weed among the city's cracks."[3]

It was then Cisneros learned something important about herself. For the first time she realized she was different. Her experiences were her own. As Cisneros later looked back at her time in Iowa she said, "I knew I was a Mexican woman."[4] She did not realize that was why she felt so out of place in Iowa. But it was her race, gender, and class that made her feel as if she did not belong.[5]

"That's when I decided I would write about something my classmates couldn't write about," Cisneros added, "[and] my writing acquired a voice."[6]

Author Sandra Cisneros sports a tattoo of the Virgin of Guadalupe, a very important religious and cultural image to the Mexican people. She once felt that her Mexican heritage made her an outsider. Now, her experiences as a nontraditional Mexican-American woman give a unique voice to her writing, which transcends cultural boundaries.

Sandra Cisneros began to write in her own way. She wanted to write a book that was as unique as she was. It would not be like any book she had checked out of a library or read in school.

She started by writing about her childhood memories. She used language she heard every day in her neighborhood. She used words everyone there used. She mixed English with Spanish words and phrases. Her narrator was a young, poor Mexican-American girl.

Cisneros graduated from the University of Iowa in 1978. She took a job as a counselor at a Latino high school in Chicago. By then, she had already written several short stories.

As she worked at her new job, she listened to the stories the students told her about their lives. She used bits of their stories in the stories she wrote. She took parts of their memories and cut and pasted them together. Cisneros created stories that were like a collage. She changed the past to fit the present. She wrote and rewrote.

Slowly a book called *The House on Mango Street* grew. The stories in the book could be read alone. They could also be read together, telling one big story. Cisneros explained that each story added "to the whole—like beads in a necklace."[7]

In 1982, she sold her idea for *The House on Mango Street* to Arte Público Press. The publisher gave her a deadline. As the date to complete the book drew near, Cisneros had trouble writing. She was afraid she could not meet her deadline. She asked for more time and then decided she needed a change. Cisneros thought she might write better in a new place. She wanted to go to Europe, but she had no money to travel abroad. Later that year, she won a grant from the National Endowment for the Arts. With money from the grant, she moved to Greece and got back to work on her book.

Cisneros met her new deadline. She sent her manuscript to the publisher on November 30, 1982. But she was still not done. Her editor asked for revisions. She spent the next two years rewriting. Revisions were completed in 1984. Now, all she could do was wait. *The House on Mango Street* was published later that year.

The book is a series of short stories. Esperanza Cordero is the main character. She is a young Mexican-American girl growing up in a Chicago *barrio*, or neighborhood. The stories help readers understand how people lived their lives in the barrio. Esperanza, whose name means hope, does not like her poor neighborhood and wants to move away. She hopes for a better life.

With the help of her young character, Cisneros identifies what she calls "the thing without a name."[8] It is a feeling of shame. The feeling that Esperanza is not good enough. Esperanza takes a hard look at these feelings. Then she learns to take pride in being herself.

By the end of the book, Esperanza finds a way to leave her house on Mango Street. But another character shares an important message with her. She must never forget who she is and where she came from. "You will

The House on Mango Street

This is the way Esperanza described the first house she lived in on Mango Street:

It's small and red with tight steps in front and windows so small you'd think they were holding their breath. Bricks are crumbling in places, and the front door is so swollen you have to push hard to get in. There is no front yard, only four little elms the city planted by the curb. Out back is a small garage for the car we don't own yet and a small yard that looks smaller between the two buildings on either side. There are stairs in our house, but they're ordinary hallway stairs, and the house has only one washroom. Everybody has to share a bedroom—Mama and Papa, Carlos and Kiki, me and Nenny.[9]

She does not think of it as a real house. It is not one she can be proud of.

always be Esperanza. You will always be Mango Street. You can't erase what you know. You can't forget who you are."[10]

Before *The House on Mango Street* was published in 1984, few people had heard of Sandra Cisneros. Her book changed that. The collection of short stories quickly became popular. The author watched as families bought her book. Many of them had little money to spend on extras. Buying a book often meant they had to wait to buy other things they might need. More than two million copies have sold since it was published. Fans brought copies of Cisneros's book when they came to signings. She was flattered by the raggedy state of the copies. She knew they had been read again and again.

Cisneros wrote *The House on Mango Street* so everyone could enjoy it. She wrote it for high-school students, for mothers, and taxi drivers. "I tried to write in simple language, so that all ages could read it," she said.[11] During the years, she has heard from many of her readers. They are of all ages and colors. They tell Cisneros how the book made them feel they could change their lives—take control. They often tell her that she has written their story. "That just gives me *escalofrios*, you know, shivers," she says.[12]

Her readers usually ask Cisneros the same two questions: Are these stories true? Are you Esperanza? She always answers, "*Sí pero no*—Yes, but no."[13] She tells them that the setting is real. She used places from her Chicago neighborhood. The feeling of shame is also something that was real.

But most of her characters are fictional. They are bits and pieces of many people she has known and talked to. Minerva, one character in the story, writes poems on little pieces of paper. She is modeled after one of Cisneros's students. Another character named Sally is pieces of different people. Part of this character is a girl Cisneros knew as a child, the other a student she taught.[14]

The stories also drew on experiences of her mother and grandmother. Cisneros included bits of stories she heard from them in her book. She honored them, by using their names. Esperanza's last name is Cordero, Cisneros's mother's maiden name. Lucy Anguiano was named for her maternal grandmother.

The House on Mango Street helped Cisneros grow as a writer. Through her stories, she learned to speak out loud. She learned to laugh. She used language she heard every day, yet she wrote with a voice all her own.

Her book is now recognized as a coming-of-age classic.[15] Cisneros did not know how important her story was when she started writing. But at some point she realized she had something special to share. She knew then that the message in *The House on Mango Street* would be read by many generations. She said, "I felt it in my heart, so I knew it was true."[16]

2

In the Barrio

From the day she was born, Sandra Cisneros was unique. She was the only daughter of Alfredo and Elvira Cisneros. Sandra was born in Chicago, Illinois, on December 20, 1954. She was their third child. The Cisneros family continued to grow. Sandra soon had six brothers.

Her father's name was Alfredo Cisneros del Moral. He was born and raised in Mexico City, Mexico. He and his parents lived like most other middle-class families. Alfredo's father wanted his son to be successful. He saved money so his son could go to college. In the 1940s, Cisneros del Moral enrolled at the university. He was very good at math and decided to be an accountant. But he did not spend enough time studying and failed his classes during his first year. Cisneros del Moral knew his father would be disappointed. He did not want to face his anger, so he ran away. He went north across the border. He entered the United States without the official papers required by the government.[1]

For awhile Cisneros del Moral lived in Philadelphia, Pennsylvania. Then, he was arrested. He was an undocumented immigrant, and the police gave him a choice. He could go back to Mexico. That would mean facing his father. Or he could join the U.S. Army and go to war.

Alfredo Cisneros decided he would rather go to war. He joined the army. For his service during World War II, he became a citizen of the United States. When the war ended, he decided to move to California. Cisneros knew he would find other Mexican Americans there. They spoke his language. He had learned only a little English in the army. He used Spanish as much as possible.

Cisneros and his brother traveled west by bus. Segregation was law in many parts of the United States in 1945. African Americans had to sit in the back of the bus separated from white citizens. This law confused the

Father's Family History

Alfred Cisneros del Moral's family had once been wealthy. However, family members had lost most of their money by gambling. Cisneros del Moral's father was a soldier. He fought in the Mexican Revolution and retired from service with a pension.

Cisneros del Moral remembered one story he heard often growing up. His great-grandfather was a talented piano player. He had once played for the president of Mexico.

two brothers.[2] Their skin was not white. It was not black. They were brown. Where were they supposed to sit?

Their bus stopped in Chicago. Cisneros decided to get off. He wanted to visit the big city. While he was there, he met his wife-to-be at a dance and decided to stay.

Elvira Cordero's family came from Mexico. The family lived a simple life. Her father worked very hard. Her mother took care of the home and the family.

Elvira's father left Mexico for the United States in 1910 to escape the Mexican Revolution. The people living in small villages were caught in the middle of the fighting. He found a job with the railroad in Chicago. He saved his money, then sent for his wife and her relatives. They came north to live with him.

Elvira was born in the United States. She was a bright girl. She loved to read and to learn. But her parents did not encourage her to finish high school. They thought Mexican girls did not need an education. They expected Elvira to grow up and be like her own mother. She would live at home until she married. Then her job would be to care for her husband and family. This was not the life Elvira wanted. She showed her independence even as a young girl. Her parents would put her to bed. But after everyone else was asleep, Elvira would climb out the window.[3]

As she grew older though, Elvira accepted the role her parents chose for her. It was important to her family.

Alfredo and Elvira married. Their first home was in a

barrio. It was one of Chicago's poorest neighborhoods. Many other Spanish-speaking families lived there.

Alfredo upholstered furniture. He worked for his uncle Perico. His uncle taught Alfredo the trade. Elvira also had a job. She worked in a factory. Neither of them made much money.

The couple raised seven children. Their second daughter, who was born after Sandra, died as a baby. So Sandra grew up the only girl among six brothers. Sandra often wished her sister had lived. She wondered if they would have been good friends.

Sandra grew up as part of a large, loving family. All

Cisneros holds up a family picture. Her mother, Elvira, is standing on the left. Although there was never enough room in the house or a lot of money in their bank accounts, the one thing the Cisneros family had a great abundance of was love for one another.

the children grew up speaking two languages. They spoke English to their mother. They spoke Spanish to their father. The family ate both traditional Mexican food and American favorites. The children were taught to work hard, to make a better life. They learned the importance of family.

But even with six brothers, Sandra was often lonely.[4] The boys ignored her most of the time. They paired up and played together. She was left out. Her brothers also tried to boss her around. They expected her to mind them, to serve the men in the family. Sandra often felt like she had "seven fathers."[5] She later explained why she liked to sit alone and write, saying, "I am the only daughter in a family of six sons. . . . That explains everything."[6]

When her brothers did notice her, it was often to tease her. They told her she was not a real Cisneros. Someday she would grow up and get married. Then she would take her husband's name.

Alfredo Cisneros missed Mexico. He also missed his mother, who still lived there. He was her favorite child. The family often made trips from Chicago to Mexico City. They gave up their rented apartment. They loaded the station wagon with their suitcases, packed bologna sandwiches to eat along the way, and headed south.[7]

Sandra was shy. She did not make friends easily.[8] The moves back and forth were painful for her. In Mexico, she was not considered a Mexican because of her American

Families in the Barrio

Most Anglos, or white people, called everyone who spoke Spanish *Hispanic*, a term that refers to people from Spain. Alfredo and Elvira's families came from Mexico, a country Spain had conquered. The Cisneros men referred to themselves as Latinos. Female family members were called Latinas. This let others know that their families had come from Central or Latin America. Sandra Cisneros refers to herself using different terms. She explains why, saying, "I usually say Latina, Mexican-American or American Mexican, and in certain contexts, Chicana, depending on whether my audience understands the term or not."[9]

ways. And in the United States, she was not accepted as an American.

Her family always returned to Chicago from Mexico. Each time they had to find a new place to rent. The apartments were always too small. Sandra remembered that the children slept "on the living room couch and fold out Lazy Boy, and on beds set up in the middle room, where the only place with any privacy was the bathroom."[10]

All these moves also meant that the children had to change schools. Each time Alfredo Cisneros would go to the parish priest. He would ask to pay reduced tuition because of the family's low income. He always told the priest he had *siete hijos*, seven sons. Cisneros wrote later that her father meant seven children. But she heard this again and again. Sandra felt left out. She "could feel [her] self being erased and would tug [her] father's sleeve and whisper: 'Not seven sons. Six! And one daughter.'"[11]

"The moving back and forth, the new school, were very upsetting to me as a child," she said. She felt more at home sitting in a tree than with another child. "I always felt connected to the trees in Chicago. . . . I felt when I was a child that trees could talk," she explained, "and I understood what they could say.'"[12] For Sandra, the trees were kind and friendly. They taught her to be patient.

Elvira Cordero had dropped out of high school. She accepted the role of a Mexican mother. She gave up many of her dreams but wanted better things for her only daughter.

Even when Sandra was growing up, an education was not considered important for Mexican-American girls. Many girls had to be little mothers to younger brothers and sisters. Sandra was one of the lucky ones. She said, "I never had to change my little brothers' diapers, I never had to cook a meal alone, nor was I ever sent to do the laundry. Certainly I had my share of housework to do as we all did, but I don't recall it interfering with my homework or my reading habits."[13]

Elvira excused Sandra from many chores around the house. She made it possible for her daughter to spend time reading and writing. Sandra needed to be alone to create. She could not write if it was noisy. If her brothers were making noise, Sandra complained to her mother.

Elvira made the boys turn off the TV. She chased them outside. Elvira defended Sandra's right to her own space from the men in the family. She encouraged her daughter to dream.

Her mother influenced Sandra in another way. She took her to the library. Even before Sandra could read, she got a library card.[14] Elvira had always liked to read and learn. She wanted to make sure Sandra did, too.

3

A House,
Not a Home

Sandra Cisneros had no sister. She had no best friend to play with. So she read. She escaped loneliness through books. Her family only owned two. One was a Bible. Her mother bought it with S&H Green Stamps. The other book was Lewis Carroll's *Alice's Adventures in Wonderland.* It was on sale at Sears.[1]

But with her library card, Sandra discovered a treasure chest. She could explore the world. As an adult, she tells everyone that she is a writer because her mother took her to the library. She looked up authors in the card catalog. She hoped someday to find her name listed there, too.

Sandra enjoyed all kinds of stories. She liked to read about people who lived long ago. She checked out books about different places. She also loved fairy tales. One of her favorites was *The Six Swans.*[2] Hans Christian Andersen wrote the tale. It is about a girl who had six brothers. All the brothers were magically turned into swans. The sister cared for her swan brothers until she broke the spell and saved them. Sandra identified with the character in *Six Swans.* They both had six brothers. There was one other connection. Her family's name, Cisneros, means "keeper of swans."

Books opened up a new world for Sandra. Soon she began to make up stories of her own. She heard a little voice in her head. It recorded events that happened in her life. The voice spoke like the narrator of a story. Sandra would hear it say: "I want you to go to the store and get me a loaf of bread and a gallon of milk. Bring back the change and don't let them gyp [cheat] you like they did last time." Then the narrator would add, "she said in a voice that was neither reproachful nor tender."[3]

This was the way Sandra began creating stories. She used her imagination to make her family's apartment, her neighborhood, and her own life more exciting.

Both Sandra's parents thought that an education was important. Her father made sure all his children studied and did their homework. He did not want them to have to work as hard as he had to. "Use this," he told them, tapping his head, "not this,"[4] showing his children his hands. Sandra later wrote about her father's work-worn hands in an article for *Glamour* magazine. She remembered how banged up they were "by a history of hammer and nails and twine and coils and springs"[5] from reupholstering furniture.

This is an illustration from one of Sandra Cisneros's favorite fairy tales by Hans Christian Andersen, *The Six Swans*. The heroine is being carried by six swans who are really her brothers put under a magic spell.

Sandra attended several Catholic schools in Chicago. There were children from different cultures in her classes. Many came from an Italian background. There were also other Latina and Latino students. But Latinos were a minority. Her teachers cared more about discipline than cultural differences.

Sandra did not thrive in this environment. She was shy and did not like to volunteer in class. "At the school I went to it was best to blend into the crowd. You didn't want to be singled out, because to be singled out was to be set up as an example or to be ridiculed," she said.[6]

Because she did not speak up, she often received poor grades. Her teachers did not encourage her to do better. If she had lived up to their expectation, Sandra believed, she would "be working in a factory, because my report card was pretty lousy. That's because I wasn't very much interested, or I was too terrified to venture or volunteer."[7]

Finally, Sandra enrolled at Saint Aloysius. The Sisters of Christian Charity ran the school. Her new teachers discovered that Sandra was a very good reader. They realized she was bright and encouraged her. She learned to study hard.

Sandra also learned to watch people. She observed events that happened around her. She recorded her feelings. Sandra started writing about what she saw when she was ten or eleven years old. She wrote at home in a spiral notebook. She kept her writing secret. The young author was afraid to share her first poems with her teachers or the other students in her class. Sandra did not think they would be interested in her experiences.

She said, "When I was 11 years old in Chicago, teachers thought if you were poor and Mexican you didn't have anything to say."[8]

In 1966, the Cisneros family borrowed money, made a down payment on a house, and moved in. Sandra was eleven. The house was a small red bungalow. It was on a run-down street called Roosevelt Road. The area, known as Humboldt Park, was on the north side of Chicago. Most of the families in the neighborhood were Puerto Rican. The house was not the one Sandra dreamed of.

She had found her dream house in a picture book, *The Little House* by Virginia Lee Burton. It was one of her favorites as a child. She read it over and over. In the story, the little house sat on a little hill, Sandra remembered, and "one family lived [there] and grew old and didn't move away."[9]

Growing Up a Chicana

Sandra watched other women and girls who lived in the barrio of Chicago. She saw her mother and other women accept their role. They were treated like second-class citizens. They had to give up dreams of their own. Wives followed rules set down by their husbands. Daughters obeyed their fathers and brothers. As Sandra observed, she soon decided that she wanted more for herself.

Some of her ideas about her dream house came from television. She watched programs like *Leave It to Beaver* and *Father Knows Best.* These families lived in houses painted white. The houses were surrounded by green lawns.

Sandra described her family's new home as "an ugly little house, bright red as if holding its breath."[10] She was ashamed of it. The new house did end the family's trips back and forth to Mexico, however.

Though Sandra hoped her family would someday move to a better house, she settled into her new neighborhood. This was important for her as a writer. Finally, she lived in a real neighborhood. She had friends and neighbors to get to know. Although she did not know it then, these real people and places would later help her create characters for her stories. Some would be part of her book *The House on Mango Street.*

When Sandra was younger, she was not aware of race or class. Now, she began to see how her life was different from the lives of others.[11] Living in her new neighborhood helped Sandra discover that she was unique. She was a Mexican American living in America. She had to adapt to two different cultures.

The Young Writer

Sandra Cisneros entered Josephinum Academy in 1968. She was thirteen years old. Like most girls her age, she was interested in boys. But Sandra was not one of the popular girls. None of her classmates asked her out on dates. She did not spend her free time with a boyfriend. Instead she read, studied hard, and continued to write.

Sandra liked high school better than grade school. Teachers recognized that she was a bright student. They encouraged her creativity. She later said, "When I was a freshman in high school . . . that's when people first realized that I could read, I could express, I could interpret the written word in a very gifted way."[1]

A high-school teacher discovered her gift quite by accident. One of the teachers asked Sandra to read a poem in class. She read it with expression and understanding and impressed her teacher and classmates. Sandra was surprised when everyone was so amazed by her oral presentation. "I didn't have any idea that it was such a big deal," she said later.[2]

Sandra had always taken her special talent to understand poetry for granted. She thought everyone could read poems the way they were supposed to be read. She grasped the writer's message easily. She thought all her classmates did, too.

During high school, Sandra discovered a favorite American poet, Emily Dickinson. Dickinson was born in 1830. She lived all her life in the town of Amherst, Massachusetts. This poet inspired Sandra to keep writing. The young Chicana was already dreaming of becoming a writer.

Sandra Cisneros as a freshman in Josephinum Academy.

Sandra often thought about the life Dickinson had lived. Dickinson had rarely traveled beyond her hometown. As she grew older, she became a recluse. She refused to leave the safety of her house and gardens. Dickinson had kept her writing secret, as Sandra did. No one knew Dickinson was a poet until her death in 1886. Then her sister discovered all her poems. She had written 1,775 poems during her lifetime. They

A Reason to Write

After *The House on Mango Street* was published, Sandra Cisneros was often invited to talk to groups of high-school students. She shared stories about her life and her experiences in school. She told them why she writes. Part of one of her talks to students was printed in the *Los Angeles Times*. She told her audience that "teachers thought if you were poor and Mexican you didn't have anything to say. Now I think what I was put on the planet for was to tell these stories."[3]

were handwritten on sheets of paper. The papers were folded and Dickinson had stitched the pages together to made booklets.

Sandra compared her life to that of Emily Dickinson. Dickinson had some advantages that Sandra did not. Dickinson had a good education. She also had a room of her own, a quiet place to create. Dickinson lived with one sister in a house that they owned. She also had enough money to live comfortably. Sandra learned that Emily Dickinson did bake and sew. But the poet did these tasks because she liked to, not because she had to. She had a housekeeper to do most of the chores.

Sandra also wondered about Dickinson's housekeeper. Did she have a secret dream? Did she wish she could study? Did she want to be more than a housekeeper?

Sandra compared Dickinson's servant to her mother,

Inspiration

Cisneros once said: "Emily Dickinson . . . was very much a homebody, but she was very connected to . . . nature. She looked at small things to see the universe: a bumblebee, a flower."[4]

Elvira, who was the Cisneros family's cook and housekeeper. She could make a dinner for nine with a budget of five dollars. Elvira was always interested in learning and in the arts. She could sing opera lyrics. She could draw and tell stories. Sandra knew that her mother would have loved to go college. But Elvira's only college education came from reading the books her children brought home from the university. Her mother had given up her dreams to take care of the family. Instead, Elvira encouraged her daughter's creativity. She encouraged Sandra to express ideas through poetry as Emily Dickinson had.

During high school, Sandra remembered that she did more reading than writing. Reading books was an important first step for her. "I was reading and reading, nurturing myself with books like vitamins, only I didn't even know it then."[5]

Sandra wrote her first poems when she was ten years old. Then Sandra did not write poetry again until her sophomore year of high school. That year the school hired a new English teacher. The new teacher was a writer. She taught students about the writing style of modern poets. She had her students read poetry. She also asked them

Cisneros felt she had much in common with the nineteenth-century American poet Emily Dickinson (1830–1886).

Young Writer

Several twists and turns helped Sandra become a poet and writer. Her own words describe two important influences while she was growing up. She claims to be a writer today because "my mother let me stay in my room reading and studying. Perhaps because she didn't want me to inherit her sadness and her rolling pin."

"I didn't marry my first boyfriend, that pest who never gave me any time alone . . . and who couldn't understand my desire to be a writer."[6]

Sandra Cisneros as a senior in Josephinum Academy.

to write poems of their own. Cisneros recalled later that her high-school poems "were filled with pleas for peace and saving the environment. Here and there I threw in a few catchy words like ecology and Coca-Cola."[7]

Her teacher also encouraged Sandra to read the poems she had written to the class. Sandra was not one of the popular crowd, but her fellow students listened to her poetry. They liked what she had to say. Her classmates'

As a senior at Josephinum, Sandra, pictured here at the top left, served as editor of the school's literary journal. Her reputation as a gifted writer grew.

positive responses encouraged Sandra. She continued to write and soon was known as the school's resident poet.

During her senior year in high school, Sandra was the editor of Josephinum's creative-writing journal. When she was not putting her thoughts and feelings down on paper, Sandra was composing stories and poems in her head. She enjoyed playing around with sounds and words. She also learned to be a collector. She gathered facts, names, character traits, and events. The bits and pieces of information she collected turned up in her poems and stories. She imitated the other poets and authors. She was a writer in training because she had not discovered a voice she could call her own.

A "Wacky" Voice
All Her Own

Sandra Cisneros graduated from high school in 1972. She was different from many other young women who lived in the barrio. She wanted to go to college. Sandra was afraid though that her family would think it was a silly idea.

She knew her father and brothers had certain expectations for girls who were only seventeen years old. They thought Sandra should live at home until she married and had a family of her own to care for. They wanted her to be just like her mother. They expected her to be a traditional Mexican-American woman. Those were the women, Cisneros said, who "lay their necks on the threshold waiting for the ball and chain."[1]

When Cisneros announced that she wanted to go to college, her brothers made fun of her. But her father's reaction was a surprise. Alfredo Cisneros thought it was a good idea. Sandra realized later that he sent her to college to find someone to marry. Her father did not think she needed an education.

"In retrospect, I'm lucky my father believed daughters were meant for husbands," Cisneros said. "It meant it didn't matter if I majored in something silly like English."[2] Her father allowed her to study whatever she wanted. It did not have to be something practical. He did not expect her to work at a career to support herself. Sandra could follow her dreams. She still wanted to be a writer so she decided to major in English.

Cisneros earned a scholarship. She enrolled at Loyola University. The college, run by the Roman Catholic Church, was in Chicago. Only a few Latina students attended the university. Cisneros realized that she was different from most of her classmates. Their families paid for their tuition. Many drove sports cars and wore designer clothes. Even though she was different, the other students accepted her. The young coed quickly discovered that she liked college.

For the first couple of years, Cisneros studied literature. The classes she took covered the works of great writers. Her professors assigned the classics. They also asked students to read modern books. The authors of these books were thought to be important examples to study. Cisneros soon noticed that most of these works had something in common. They were written by white males. There was one exception to that rule. Students were also expected to read and study the poetry of Emily Dickinson.

Other Students

Sandra Cisneros saw another side to students who had more money than she did. In her opinion, they had few responsibilities. They had no understanding of how others had to struggle to get by. They could drive by tenement apartments of Chicago and not even see the poor who lived there.

"When I think those kids are now the people changing history," Cisneros said, "the ones in government . . . making our laws, it makes me sad. . . . [They have] no understanding of how hard it is to rise above harsh circumstance—like speaking another language."[3]

But in many ways, Cisneros felt she had an advantage over those classmates. She could write about "worlds they never dream of, of things they never could learn from a college textbook." She said, "I [have] the power to speak and [I am] privileged enough to be heard. That is a responsibility."[4]

Cisneros enjoyed all the reading she had to do. The study of great authors helped her grow as a writer. For the first two years at Loyola, she did little creative writing. Cisneros later explained that she was "busy just being a college student and getting all my requirements."[5]

During her junior year, she took a creative-writing class. The professor required students to write poetry or fiction. They shared their writing with others in the class and students critiqued one another's stories and poems. Cisneros learned many things as she listened to comments from her peers. She learned to read her own work more objectively. She looked for ways to make each piece better, reworking it again and again. She read her work out loud. She learned to listen to her own words. She also found new models for her poetry. One of her favorites was poet Donald Justice.

Cisneros was writing again, but no one noticed her creative talent immediately. She said later, "I was an English major because I didn't know what to do about my writing and my desire to be a writer. I just thought [I'd] teach high school English and write on the side. No one . . . advised me, and I was too ashamed to say that I really wanted to be a writer."[6]

Cisneros kept writing and soon others paid attention to her work. One of her instructors was a poet. He saw promise in her writing and encouraged her to apply to the University of Iowa Writers' Workshop. After giving it some thought, Cisneros decided to apply. She filled out the application and made copies of poems she felt were her best. The school accepted her application.

Cisneros graduated from Loyola in 1976 and was soon packing to move to Iowa. She was leaving Chicago. For the first time, she would be living on her own. She was a little nervous but looked forward to what she could learn in the Iowa Writers' Workshop.

Sandra Cisneros started classes at Iowa in the fall of 1976. One of the instructors was Donald Justice. Justice was a poet Cisneros had studied at Loyola. She admired his writing, but he was her instructor only for a short

Cisneros entered the University of Iowa Writers' Workshop to complete a master's degree in creative writing. The program is housed in this mid-nineteenth-century mansion known as the Dey House.

time. Justice took a leave soon after the workshop began that year.

Iowa City was very different from Chicago. Cisneros did not seem to fit in with the other students. She was lonely and for the first time really noticed her ethnic differences. She later explained how she felt: "In graduate school what I said was looked at as so wacky that you right away shut up. It didn't take me long to learn—after a few days being there—that nobody cared to hear what I had to say and no one listened to me even when I did speak. I became very frightened . . . that first year."[7]

Iowa Writers' Workshop

The University of Iowa was the first school in the United States to have a program for writers. It was a two-year program. Students study and practice creative writing there. The first session started in 1936. It became known as the Iowa Writers' Workshop. Since then, many other colleges have set up classes in creative writing. They often use the Iowa program as a model. Even today, the Iowa Writers' Workshop is considered to be one of the best for creative writing.

Cisneros again turned to books for support and encouragement. She studied the writing of others who came from different cultures. She read the books of Maxine Hong Kingston, a Chinese-American writer. She also discovered Toni Morrison, an African-American author.

Cisneros was never completely comfortable in Iowa, but she did eventually find friends. One was Joy Harjo. Harjo was a Creek Indian who had grown up in Oklahoma. Harjo also knew what it felt like to be a woman of color growing up in America. Both Cisneros and Harjo were beginning writers. They helped each other, offering support and encouragement. Today, Harjo is a published author. She is known for her poetry and her music.

Cisneros also became friends with Dennis Mathis, who wrote fiction. He was the editor who later helped Cisneros with *The House on Mango Street*.

Sandra Cisneros claimed that the Writers' Workshop

failed her, but it was through this experience that she discovered her own voice. As a child, she had learned to listen and watch others carefully. Now, she observed students in the workshop classes.

Before long, Cisneros decided there were topics she could write about that her classmates could not. These topics grew from her childhood. She had experienced poverty and cultural differences. She also understood what it felt like to be uprooted and to have men dominate her life.

Cisneros began to write from her own experience. If others wrote about swans and flowers, she did the opposite. She created ugly poetry using slang and topics that were unpleasant. One poem she created was about a rat. The first line read: "Pink as a newborn rat."[8]

The characters in her stories were poor. They had to work hard to survive. She created strong women. These women refused to follow tradition and bow to the demands of husbands. She wrote about the struggle of Latinas to adapt to a new American culture and also honor their family heritage and traditions. Cisneros's writing served a purpose. She helped others understand what it was like to be a Chicana living in America. She helped them understand what it was like to grow up and survive in the barrios. Her voice opened the doors between the two cultures she claimed.

After two years in Iowa, Cisneros graduated with a master's degree in creative writing. She had found her voice. Now, she needed to find a job.

6

Stories or "Healthy Lies"

After graduating, Cisneros moved back to Chicago. She went to work as a school counselor and teacher in 1979. Her job was at an alternative high school for Latinos. It was a school for "dropouts." The term *dropout*, though, did not always fit her students. Cisneros explained that some had left school because they had babies. Others were afraid of classmates who beat them up. She also taught kids with learning disabilities and poor study skills. Some struggled to overcome language barriers. Most were back in school for the same reason. They wanted to complete their education. They wanted to get a good job.

Working with these students was a challenge. Cisneros said she "often felt helpless . . . to alter their lives."[1] They were exposed to shocking situations. Many had witnessed drive-by shootings and armed robberies. Some had run away from home to escape abuse. Others turned to drugs or alcohol to help them forget their problems. Young girls often had three kids of their own before they were eighteen.

Her students were not good writers, but according to Cisneros, "man, could they talk a good story." These kids had earned "doctorates in the university of life." She wanted to help them understand that "they were extraordinary for having survived."[2]

As Cisneros taught, she discovered she was also learning. Her students lived in the barrio as she had. But the stories they shared gave her a more complete picture of growing up poor in Chicago. She listened to *what* they said and *how* they said it.

Cisneros often saw her own reflection in their faces. Later, she said that the girls would "laugh behind cupped hands and hunker themselves between hunched shoulders as if they could make themselves disappear."[3] Cisneros understood. She had also been a shy child who lacked confidence.

Her job as their teacher was demanding, but Cisneros made time for her own writing. She was no longer shy. She needed to express her feelings. She had already drafted some of the chapters for *The House on Mango Street.* The book had started out as a memoir. But as Cisneros learned from her students, the project changed. She collected their experiences and saved them. She took bits and pieces from their lives and mixed them with her own memories. Her book turned into a collection of stories, or as she would say, "healthy lies."[4]

Not Enough Confidence

In 1978, Cisneros graduated with a master's degree. She could have applied to teach creative writing at the college level. However, she did not feel qualified. She was Mexican-American and a woman. What did she know that could be shared with college-level students? Cisneros had earned her degree, but she did not have the confidence to apply for a teaching job at any university.

While she was teaching, Cisneros also wrote and submitted poetry. Some of her poems were published in literary journals. She read her work aloud in coffeehouses and bars. Soon people recognized her as a new talent. She was pleased with the recognition her writing received. However, teaching consumed much of her time. She did not have enough time to write, to perfect her craft.

The Chicago Transit Authority (CTA) also helped make Cisneros famous. The CTA runs the city's public transportation system. They sponsored a poetry project. With the help of the Poetry Society of America, poems were selected for display inside buses and trains. Those chosen included Gwendolyn Brooks (a poet from Chicago), Carl Sandburg (who lived in Illinois), and Sandra Cisneros. Thousands of commuters read her poems daily on their way to work. They did not know the sound of her voice, but they recognized her words.

Other writers began to take notice of Cisneros. One

of them, Gary Soto, is also a Mexican American. He realized that Cisneros was a writer who had something special to say. He helped edit *Bad Boys*, her first book. It was a poetry collection published in 1980. Mango Press in San Jose, California, printed less than one thousand copies. Her poems described the Chicago barrio of her childhood. The voice rang true, and Cisneros's audience enjoyed the strong images she painted.

Cisneros quit teaching about the time *Bad Boys* was published. She needed a job that allowed more time for writing. She went to work for Loyola University, the college from which she had graduated. This job also kept her in touch with Latino students. She was a recruiter. It was her responsibility to talk to high-school students from

A train at the CTA Station. Commuters read Cisneros's work displayed inside Chicago's trains and buses.

Chicano author Gary Soto

the barrio. Cisneros did her best to encourage kids to enroll at the university. But she also understood why many would never attend college. Lack of money was only one issue. Many families did not feel college was important, especially for young women. Little had changed in the Mexican-American culture. Girls were still expected to grow up, get married, and raise a family.

By this time, Cisneros had had a few steady boyfriends, but she was not ready to get married. Her first serious boyfriend was Anglo, or Caucasian. He asked Cisneros to marry him and share his dream of a house in the suburbs. She saw problems with the relationship and said no.

The young poet was concerned that marriage would interfere with her writing. She needed time alone to craft poems and stories. Her boyfriend did not understand this. He also did not understand her desire to achieve something for Latinas. She knew "he wasn't Mexican, didn't grow up poor, and had no ambition to be/do anything in his life other than buy that house, put his feet up and sigh."[5]

As she continued to write, her own style developed. She pulled from the two languages of her childhood. Most of her text was in English, but she used Spanish words and phrases, too. Cisneros did not define the Spanish words. Definitions interrupted the rhythm of her words, she explained, and left "the seams showing."[6] Readers must use context to understand the meaning.

She applied this style to her new project, *The House on Mango Street*. Cisneros had written several short stories: "Alicia Who Sees Mice," "Sally," and "What Sally Said." She began to see these stories as chapters in a book.

Lazy Poems

Chapters in *The House on Mango Street* read like poetry. They are filled with sharp images, sounds, and metaphors. Cisneros called her stories "lazy poems."[7] If she had worked longer with each chapter, the end result would have been a poem. She decided to write chapters instead, not because she was lazy, but because she believed her message was stronger as a story.

She looked honestly at the real problems of barrios. She wrote *Mango Street* "as a reaction against those . . . who want to make barrios look like Sesame Street, or some place warm and beautiful."[8] But the people who live there know better. They live with piles of garbage on the street, drive-by shootings, rats, and rundown apartments. Cisneros's lazy poems helped others understand.

Now, Cisneros needed time to focus on her writing and complete the project.

That was a problem. Cisneros had to work to make money to live. A regular job took time away from her writing. Finally, in 1982, the young author found a solution. She received a grant from the National Endowment for the Arts (NEA). As soon as she could, the twenty-seven-year-old quit her job and focused on writing.

Cisneros also got something else she needed—encouragement. The support came from publisher Nick Kanellos. He ran a small press called Arte Público. Kanellos edited one of Cisneros's short stories. He realized that she had talent and encouraged her to keep working. Cisneros took his advice. She also worked out a deal with Arte Público. They agreed to publish *The House on Mango Street* when it was finished. Now, she had a deadline to work toward.

Nick Kanellos, director of Arte Público Press. When it published *The House on Mango Street* in the 1980s, it was small and relatively unknown. Now, Arte Público is one of the country's oldest and largest Latino publishers, thanks in part to the success of Cisneros's novel.

First Cisneros decided to change her own environment. She left Chicago and moved to Provincetown, Massachusetts. Friend and fellow writer Dennis Mathis lived there. He had been her "best buddy" while she was in graduate school in Iowa. Mathis also wrote fiction. He offered to help Cisneros.

Cisneros appreciated her friend's guidance. She later wrote: "He was my editor for what I feel are the cleanest pieces in the book."[9] Mathis worked with Cisneros on several *Mango Street* chapters, including "My Name," "Hips," "Elenita," "Cards," "Palm," and "Water." Her days now were filled with writing and rewriting. Time went by quickly. Though she could devote all her time to her writing, Cisneros was worried. It was almost time to submit her completed manuscript. She did not think her novel was ready. She was afraid she would not meet the deadline.

Chicana Around the World

Once her editor at Arte Público agreed to extend her deadline, Cisneros decided she needed a change of scenery. She thought living someplace new might help her writing. She had some money from the NEA grant. So she packed her bags and bought a ticket to Greece. On the date of her first deadline, she was on her way.

Living on the Aegean Sea in Greece did seem to help. Cisneros went back to work on her story. She finished the manuscript in time to meet the new deadline. On November 30, 1982, she submitted the completed draft to Kanellos.

Kanellos read the entire manuscript carefully. He thought it was good but not as good as it could be. Editors often ask authors to make revisions on manuscripts and he suggested that Cisneros continue to work on her stories. With more work, Kanellos felt the stories would be more focused and forceful. Cisneros agreed with him. She moved to France and then got back to work. It took two more years for her to complete *The House on Mango Street.*

As Cisneros focused on revisions, she also spent time on other projects. In the spring of 1983, she once again needed money so she could continue to write and to eat. She accepted a position in Venice, Italy. She worked as an artist-in-residence at the Michael Karolyi Foundation.

This worked out well for Cisneros. As an artist-in-residence, she taught only a few hours each week. In return, the school paid for her room and board. While Cisneros taught a few classes and lectured, she still had time to work on her own writing projects. By now, she was designing a second book project. It would be a collection of poems, covering a wide variety of topics. Several poems described loves—lost and found. She had selected the title *My Wicked Wicked Ways.* Her new project, revisions on *Mango Street,* and teaching filled her days.

Cisneros also traveled around Europe. She wanted to learn about other countries and the people who lived there. She was interested in different cultures. Wherever she went, Cisneros discovered how much she had in common with women of other nationalities. They had to work hard to support themselves and have careers, just as she did. Cisneros understood their day-to-day struggle. They needed money for the basics—food, shelter, and clothing.

During the short time in Europe, Cisneros became friends with women that she met. No matter what country they lived in, these women seemed to share her values. They treated one another with respect and honor. They made her feel at home. Cisneros later explained that these "women helped me and they asked for nothing in return, and they gave me great compassion and love when I was feeling lost and alone."[1]

In 1983, Cisneros moved to Yugoslavia. During the summer, she worked in a garden shared with neighbors. That was where she met one of her closest friends. Jasna was a Yugoslav woman. From the first moment they met, Cisneros felt a deep connection to her. The two women liked and understood each other.

Cisneros and Jasna helped each other find supplies needed to take care of the household. They shared stories. Soon, Cisneros felt Jasna was like the sister she had never had. It was as if they had known each other forever.

Cisneros's travels in Europe helped her understand several cultures. She realized that all people struggling against poverty shared similar problems. She made herself a

A Different Way of Life

Living in Yugoslavia was quite an experience, especially for an American. Yugoslavia was a Communist country. Many products used all the time in the United States were unavailable or difficult to find. It was a struggle to find basics like toilet paper. There were no corner grocery stores or drug stores.

promise. She would use her voice and her words to help the poor, to help people of color, and to help women. With her writing, she would speak out on issues that spoke to her heart.

In 1984, Cisneros completed *The House on Mango Street*. She was twenty-nine years old. She had spent two years working on revisions. During that time, she had grown as a writer and a person. She was ready to submit it again. She sent the manuscript to Kanellos. It would be several months before her book would be in print. Now, all she could do was wait and worry.

She was concerned about book reviews. What would the critics think of her new book? What would they say about her writing? Cisneros had revised each story one at a time. Now she studied how the stories fit together to form a whole. She wanted *Mango Street* to help others see what it was like to grow up poor in the barrio. Had she accomplished what she set out to do?

Soon after her book was finished, she wrote to a friend about her concerns. She explained her feelings of "terror of having to live with *Mango Street*."[2] Cisneros recalled how each story had been pieced together, saying it was like "making a quilt by the light of a flashlight."[3] Soon, her book would be published for others to read. They would applaud or criticize her work. As the author, she would have to accept their comments, good or bad.

Cisneros returned to the United States later that year. She wanted to be there when her publisher released *The House on Mango Street*. She wanted to hear what reviewers

Words Into Other Languages

Jasna and Cisneros remained friends long after Cisneros returned to the United States. When *The House on Mango Street* was published, the young author became popular. People in other countries wanted to read her poetry and stories. Her words were printed in other languages. Jasna helped to translate some of Cisneros's writing into Serbo-Croatian. That was the language used by many people who lived in Yugoslavia.

had to say about her work. It would take a few months for them to read and comment on her book. Cisneros waited and worked on new writing projects.

Finally, the reviews were out. Most were positive. Critics praised Cisneros's work. American poet Gwendolyn Brooks wrote: "Sandra Cisneros is one of the most brilliant of today's young writers. Her work is . . . rich with music and picture."[4]

A book reviewer for the *New York Times*, Bebe Moore Campbell, made this comment: "Cisneros draws on her rich [Latino] heritage . . . creating unforgettable characters we want to lift off the page. She is not only a gifted writer, but an absolutely essential one."[5]

The *Miami Herald* called it "a deeply moving novel . . . delightful and poignant. . . . Like the best of poetry, it opens the windows of the heart without a wasted word."[6]

Not all reviewers liked *The House on Mango Street*.

A *Booklist* critic wrote that her "loose and deliberately simple style," halfway between prose and poetry, "occasionally . . . annoys by its cuteness."[7]

Other authors applauded *The House on Mango Street*. Gary Soto found her writing style interesting. He complimented Cisneros, calling her "foremost a storyteller."[8]

Many praised Cisneros for sharing the Mexican-American culture with her audience. Her character, Esperanza, helped readers relate to children and families with different backgrounds. Through her story, Cisneros showed how people of all cultures share similar hopes and concerns.

The House on Mango Street also won the Before Columbus Foundation's American Book Award in 1985. The award is presented once a year. It recognizes excellence and diversity in American writing.

Cisneros's first novel was a success. The reviews were good. She had won an important award. Unfortunately, book sales did not make her rich overnight. Her grant money was almost gone. She still could not support herself by writing. It was time to look for another job.

Tejanos
and Texas

In 1984, the Guadalupe Cultural Arts Center in San Antonio, Texas, hired Sandra Cisneros as an arts administrator. The city of San Antonio was a good fit for Cisneros. Its population was made up of many Spanish-speaking people. They had come from all over Latin America. Cisneros was more comfortable in her new home than in the Chicago neighborhood where she had grown up. She felt she belonged in San Antonio.

"Something happened when I moved to Texas," she explained, "I didn't realize that I had been searching for it in a sense, but I felt I was born in the wrong place. Maybe what happened when I came here was recognition of the light, the sky and the landscape that I remembered from my trips to Mexico as a child. . . . I felt like I had come home."[1]

Cisneros found the Spanish-speaking people in Texas different from Latinos, people from the Caribbean or

Central American countries, who lived in Chicago. Texas and Mexico share a border, and San Antonio was once part of Mexico. Many San Antonio families have lived in the United States for generations. They considered themselves Texans and had adopted the name Tejanos. That term means people of Texas with Mexican heritage.

Other Mexican Americans living in Cisneros's Chicago neighborhood had moved to the United States recently. They were often the first or second generation to live there. These families still thought of themselves as Mexicans. Many made the long trip back and forth between the two countries regularly.

Cisneros worked hard at her job and also volunteered to plan cultural events for the community. For one of these events, she invited Latino writers to the city. She asked them to share stories about their culture. She wanted people of all colors, including whites, to attend. She planned to expose non-Hispanics to the Mexican-American heritage of the area. She felt this was part of what made San Antonio a special place.

Cisneros was disappointed with the turnout.[2] Mexican Americans came, but only a few white people attended. Her plan to bring her two cultures together failed. It was a frustrating experience. It affected her attitude toward the white community.

She was especially disappointed in white, upper-class ladies. She had little sympathy for them unless they tried to understand how her world was different from theirs. She recalled later that she "didn't have any white women

A mural of the Virgin Mary on the side of the Guadalupe Cultural Arts Center where Cisneros worked as an arts administrator. This image, known as Our Lady of Guadalupe (or the Virgin of Guadalupe), represents the patron saint of Mexico.

friends when . . . in Texas."[3] She developed a racist attitude but did not like to admit it.[4]

Cisneros continued to use her voice and her writing to speak out for Chicanos. She supported women's movements, focusing her concerns on helping women of color. She became a spokesperson for their causes.

Sandra Cisneros's frustrations did not change the way she felt about her new "hometown." She loved San Antonio. She was a Chicana living with others like herself, near Mexico, the country of their roots.

Cisneros found San Antonio appealing for other reasons, too. The residents knew about the history of the area. They were proud that it once was part of Mexico. She was impressed by the people's knowledge of important events that had happened in the past.

Generally, the people living in the city valued the arts, including the arts of Mexican Americans. Cisneros also enjoyed hearing the language of Old Mexico more often. Spanish words and phrases were everywhere. Many words were used so commonly that they had been adopted as part of the English spoken in San Antonio. She listened to this mix of the two languages she had grown up with. Cisneros heard the rhythms and patterns. They became part of her writing style.

As happy as she was in San Antonio, Cisneros still had one problem—finding time to write. She liked her job. She liked the people she worked with. But being an arts administrator filled up her days.

Though *Mango Street* continued to sell, Cisneros later

Cisneros at Home in Her Heart

Two cultures, two languages thrived in San Antonio and so did Sandra Cisneros. It was a place she had searched for, like Esperanza in *The House on Mango Street*. In one story, Esperanza goes to a fortune-teller. She wants the answer to one important question: will she someday have a house of her own? She is disappointed when the fortune-teller predicts she will find "a home in her heart."

In Texas, Cisneros was luckier than Esperanza. She found a place she could call home.

told one interviewer, "I had to be a teacher, a counselor, I've had to work as an Arts Administrator, you know, all kinds of things just to make my living. The writing is always what you try to save energy for, it's your child."[5]

Then in 1985, she got the financial help she needed. Cisneros won a Dobie Paisano Fellowship. The fellowship, or grant, included a salary and a place to work. For the next six months, she lived on a ranch near Austin, Texas. It was quiet and peaceful. Cisneros could concentrate completely on her writing.

She focused on the poetry book, *My Wicked Wicked Ways*, which she had started in Europe. The poems described her travels in Europe and growing up in Chicago. Other poems discussed Cisneros's feelings of guilt. She had been raised Catholic, but she could not be the good, dutiful wife and mother her culture expected.

Her poems declared her freedom to live life her own way.

Since her first poetry book, *Bad Boys,* was out of print, she also included some of those poems in her new collection.

Cisneros made good use of the time she had to write. She completed her book and sent it off to publishers. Living on the Texas ranch suited her. She fell in love with the countryside and with the state of Texas. It "made me whole," Cisneros wrote.[6]

When the fellowship ended, Cisneros had to find another job. She returned to San Antonio, hoping to make it her permanent home. People there had begun to recognize her as a promising Chicana author. They knew her from public readings, school presentations, and her job as an arts administrator. More than five thousand copies of *The House on Mango Street* had sold and the book was now in its third printing. Unfortunately, none of this fame helped her find a job.

Ghosts

Cisneros spoke at Indiana University in November 1986. She explained that she did not wait for ideas to inspire her. Writing was something she had to do. She was driven.

When asked about subjects she wrote about, Cisneros said, "I would have to say I write about those ghosts inside that haunt me, that will not let me sleep, of that which even memory does not like to mention."[7]

Her Own Style

Her approach to teaching was unique. She tried to teach her writing students to see the stories in their own lives. She encouraged them to listen to voices around them. Voices fascinated Cisneros. She studied them and focused on how people spoke instead of the actual meaning. She said in one interview, "Wherever you put me I write about what I hear."[8] She soaked in the sounds and rhythms of words and used "the voices" in her writing.

As a last resort, Cisneros offered writing workshops. She passed out fliers in supermarkets. She tacked signs up on street posts, trying to get students to fill her classes. Not enough people signed up.

In the fall of 1987, California State University, Chico offered her a position teaching creative writing. Cisneros had no other options. She packed up and borrowed money to get there. She left Texas, the place she had called home.

It was Cisneros's first time teaching at a university. She found it uncomfortable, saying, "I was in a new city, I did not know anyone; I was in a new job with just a lot of pressure to succeed, and I put a lot of demands on myself. I felt I had to be perfect."[9]

It is common for creative writing professors to work on their own projects during their spare time. Cisneros could not do that. She gave all her time to her teaching. If her students failed, she felt like a failure.

She also found it difficult to plan lessons that would fit within the scheduled class time. She did not like to end a class before the students had finished writing. She was uncomfortable when students had to put down their pens, sometimes in mid-sentence.

Cisneros struggled with other time-related issues. She found it difficult to work within a schedule. She often arrived late to class. Her students resented this. They had to get to class on time. Their instructor should not keep them waiting.

Cisneros thought about quitting, but she would need to borrow money again if she left. She did not want to do that. She felt trapped. She later described this as "the worst year of [her] life."[10]

While Cisneros was teaching in Chico, literary agent Susan Bergholz called. She wanted to talk to Cisneros about a new book contract. Cisneros would not return

Nightmare to Poetry

While teaching in Chico, Cisneros had a nightmare. She remembered it well because she dreamed in Spanish. She woke up and told herself, "*Tantas cosas asustan, tantas*," meaning "So many things terrify, so many." That was how she felt at the time.[11]

These words became the title of a poem. She wrote the poem in Spanish, not a mix of her two languages. When asked why, she replied. "When I tried to translate it into English, it sounded wrong to me and I had to leave it in Spanish."[12]

the agent's calls. She felt lost. She did not believe she was good as a teacher. She had no confidence in her writing.

She could not shake feelings of depression. She even thought briefly of killing herself.[13] But she quickly realized that was foolish, remembering what she told a junior-high audience in 1986, "I don't want to die young. I don't want to drive fast, or get on airplanes, or sit with my back to the door when I'm in a bar. For the sake of my writing I want a long life."[14]

Cisneros was living with a friend, Norma Alarcon. Alarcon was also an editor. She encouraged Cisneros to keep writing no matter how she felt. Cisneros tried. She finished another collection of poems but then was too depressed to start any other projects.

Finally, some good news arrived. A small publisher called. Cisneros had submitted the collection of poems she had completed during her fellowship in Texas to them. Third Woman Press wanted to publish *My Wicked Wicked Ways.*

Time to Write

Cisneros often called 1987 the worst year of her life. But three things happened before it ended, making it possibly her best year. First, *My Wicked Wicked Ways* was published. The interesting title reflected Cisneros's view of herself. She had learned to make her own decisions, taking control of her life. This was not the usual role for a woman raised Catholic and Mexican. She believed that others from her background would see her choices as something "wicked."

Second, she received another grant from the National Endowment for the Arts. The award was what Cisneros needed. It renewed her confidence in herself. She now had the time and money to get back to her own writing. She quit teaching and began to work full-time on a new project. It was a collection of short stories called *Woman Hollering Creek and Other Stories*.

Finally, the author took another big step. She made a

phone call to Susan Bergholz. The agent had been trying to contact her for several years. After the two talked, Cisneros sent Bergholz some of her new stories. The agent liked the thirty-nine pages she read. She began to send them out to editors at publishing houses.

Cisneros was pleased with her new agent's approach to publishing. In an interview published later, Cisneros said that Bergholz wanted to "sell books to the best place that a book could go to [even] if that meant a small publishing house or less money."[1]

Within months, Bergholz sold *Woman Hollering Creek and Other Stories.* Random House/Vintage Press bought the collection. The stories were about strong Mexican-American women living along the Texas-Mexico border. Cisneros set records with this sale. She became the first Chicana to receive a major publishing contract for a work about Chicanas. She also received the largest advance ever made to a Mexican-American writer up to that time.[2]

The contract with a highly respected publisher boosted Cisneros's career. She called it her "green card," slang for a registration card that allows citizens of other countries to live and work in the United States.[3] It was like a pass. It gave her permanent status as a Chicana writer in America. This book contract brought other changes, too. Now, she could live in San Antonio. She could write full-time and not worry about money.

She could also use her writing skills to fulfill an important purpose. She voiced this goal in 1986 during a

Agent Seeks Author

Agent Susan Bergholz read *The House on Mango Street*. She liked it and wanted to represent the new Chicana author. She decided to track Cisneros down. That was something she had never done before. "It was a delightful chase," Bergholz recalls.[4] She made phone calls and talked to Richard Bray of Guild Bookstore. He knew Cisneros and passed the agent's message on to her. Even with his help, "the chase" took three to four years. When Bergholz and Cisneros finally spoke, they agreed to work together.

presentation to junior-high students. Cisneros stated that she wanted to become an author who wrote on behalf of those lacking power. She wanted to express "the words of thousands of silent women" so that "their stories can finally be heard."[5]

The large advance from Random House created enormous pressure. Cisneros had to meet their deadline. She had been writing one story every six months. She would have to work faster. Fearing she might not finish on time, Cisneros worked eight to twelve hours every day. "There's nothing like a deadline to teach you discipline, especially when you've already spent your advance," she said. "Before, I'd be scratching my *nalgas* [behind], waiting for inspiration. Now I know I can work this hard. I know I did the best I could."[6] Writing for so many hours was exhausting. But Cisneros was pleased with what she accomplished.

Cisneros valued her privacy while working on *Woman Hollering Creek.* She set up a routine. She tried different ways to keep herself focused. She would light candles, pray, or read from favorite books.[7] Sometimes the writing was a struggle. She simply had to force herself to put words on the page. At other times, she dreamed she was her character, and telling the story was as easy as talking to a friend.

Cisneros polished story after story. Her hard work paid off. The characters blossomed into strong women and girls with messages to share. She showed how the struggles of women living in the barrio gave them strength, helping them reach their hopes and dreams. Strong female characters tied her collection of stories together.

Her new collection expanded the themes found in *The House on Mango Street.* She dug deeply into life in the barrio. She added new characters ranging from migrant farmworkers to college graduates. Cisneros included as many different voices as possible. She wanted America to learn all it could about Chicanas who share this country.

The book was published in 1991 and critics praised *Woman Hollering Creek and Other Stories.* Cisneros drew story ideas from Latin American mythology, but changed the male characters in the original tales to females. These revisions, Cisneros explained, empowered women to rethink history.

When Sandra Cisneros was a child she did not

Sandra Cisneros in 1991, shortly after the publication of *Woman Hollering Creek and Other Stories*.

have many friends and hated being alone. Now, the adult writer enjoyed having time and space for herself. Cisneros did not want anything or anyone to take that away from her.

She decided to dedicate her life to her writing. She would not marry or have a family. Her poems and stories would be her children. Cisneros tried to explain her decision to her own family, but they could not understand her need for solitude. In defense of her decision, Cisneros said that she had never met a married couple who were as happy together as she was alone.

Her poem, entitled "Old Maids," talks about this issue. The poem unfolds as single women attend a friend's wedding. They are asked when they will marry. The answer: "We don't marry. We're *too old* by Mexican standards."[8] The narrator puzzles about what might have happened to discourage them from becoming wives. The poem also asks married women to look at their lives. Are they really as happy as they think they are?

For the time being, Cisneros was contented with her decision. She liked living alone. She could do what she wanted. Sometimes, she turned her music up and danced around the house alone. It was her way of celebrating the fact that she had a house of her own and only herself to take care of.

After the publication of *Woman Hollering Creek*, Cisneros won The Lannan Literary Award for Fiction. It is given each year for exceptional works. Part of this prize was a grant.

Poetry or Fiction

Cisneros often makes surprising discoveries as she works on poetry. She once said that "[w]hen you think: 'Oh my goodness, I didn't know I felt that!' that's where you stop. That's the little piece of gold."[9] As she composes lines for a poem, she looks for that surprising idea, and does not think about her audience.

Her approach to writing fiction is different. Before she begins, she knows what she wants to write and where the story is going. For her, a story has to be "something someone wants to listen to."[10] She always keeps her readers in mind when writing fiction.

Cisneros took little time to celebrate her success. She had to get back to work on a new book. She had received another large advance for *Loose Woman* from Turtle Bay Books. The publisher also planned to reprint *My Wicked Wicked Ways*. The original publisher, Third Woman Press, was no longer in business.

By 1992, Cisneros had made a name for herself. She could support herself with books, lectures, and tours. One reporter suggested that she had become a success overnight. This made Cisneros laugh. She called her overnight success "the longest night [she'd] ever spent."[11] It had been a struggle that took fifteen long years.

The publication of *Woman Hollering Creek* was also an important first in the publishing industry. Cisneros was now recognized as a mainstream author, an author who was among the most popular. This meant that her books would reach the hands of many more readers.

In an interview on National Public Radio, Cisneros commented on her success as a Chicano writer. "I think I can't be happy if I'm the only one that's getting published by Random House when I know there are such magnificent writers—both Latinos and Latinas, both Chicanos and Chicanas—in the U.S. whose books are not published by mainstream presses or whom the mainstream isn't even aware of."[12] She hoped her book's success would change that situation. She wanted to share the spotlight with other talented women of color. She hoped that it would encourage publishers to seek out and support other writers like herself.

Now, Cisneros had no doubts about her future. She had returned to San Antonio and planned to make it her permanent home. She decided it was time to buy a house of her own. She found just what she was looking for in a nice neighborhood. It was a small Victorian house with its own backyard. It was a place she could live and write comfortably. She said in an interview: "I feel as if my house is this boat and I'm docked in this little green sea. I don't have to leave . . . my property to feel close to nature."[13] She had come home.

Cisneros also made another purchase about this time. She bought a bright red pickup truck. She hung fringe around the windshield and decorated it to suit herself. The purchase of the truck impressed her father. It was something he could relate to. Finally, he was convinced that his daughter had become a successful author. At last, he took his only daughter and her writing seriously.

Though San Antonio was home, Cisneros continued to travel. She went on tour to publicize new projects and *The House on Mango Street*. It had been republished by Vintage Books, a major publishing company. They funded readings to promote book sales and name recognition for Cisneros.

In 1992, Cisneros traveled to Mexico with other Latino writers. These authors attended the 1992 Feria Internacional del Libro, the Guadalajara International Book Fair. Their goal was to introduce their writing to Mexican and Latin American readers.

Cisneros was part of a panel at the conference. American writers discussed their work. When she spoke, Cisneros pointed out what she considered to be a sad fact. She was the only Chicana in the world who could support herself with her writing. Cisneros sent a message to the publishers attending the conference. She challenged them to find more women writers like herself. She challenged them to publish their work, too.

Sandra Cisneros visits Norcross High School in Georgia in 2009, the twenty-fifth anniversary of *The House on Mango Street*. Despite her hectic schedule, Cisneros finds time to reach out to her readers.

10

Speaking Out

By now, people knew the name Sandra Cisneros. Her poems and stories were included in textbooks used across the country. She was a respected writer, proud to take a stand on issues she felt were important. Cisneros focused on problems experienced by Latinos, but she did not forget other ethnic groups and their concerns. She set an example with her own actions. She urged other writers to speak out, too. She encouraged them to work to heal their communities, explaining that they had the power to set change in motion.

To begin, they had to spotlight that pain for their readers. Cisneros also stressed the importance of building a community. She encouraged her audience to look around them. To take note of people who performed necessary jobs like custodians and garbage collectors. These people work for little pay and often receive little appreciation.

Balancing Act

Sandra Cisneros grew up with two cultures. She described this experience as a balancing act. She tried to be both Mexican and American. But sometimes that did not work. Some who shared her Mexican culture believed it was bad to try to be like Americans.

And because she was Chicana, Americans often did not accept her as one of them. She felt rejected by both cultures. Her writing helped her deal with the feeling that she did not belong. It helped her figure out who she was as a person and what she wanted to do with her life.

One of Cisneros's jobs as an author was to promote her books by touring the country. She spoke to groups of students, writers, and book lovers about her work. She discussed what it is like to be a Mexican-American woman growing up in America. Cisneros explained how it felt to live in-between. "We're always straddling two countries . . . but not belonging to either culture. In some sense we're not Mexican and in some sense we're not American. I couldn't live in Mexico because my ideas are too . . . Americanized. On the other hand I can't live in America, or I do live here but, in some ways almost like a foreigner."[1]

Cisneros tried to adapt to both her cultures. Sometimes other Chicanos accused her of selling out. They thought she wanted to fit in with the white community, forgetting her Mexican heritage. But she proved her critics wrong in 1992. The Gap, a popular clothing store chain, asked Cisneros to do commercials. Starring in the commercials would have made her a celebrity. The company offered her a great deal of money to advertise for their store. Cisneros said no. She would have been the first Chicana to star in The Gap ads. However, she would have felt like a traitor to her ethnic group if she had done the commercials. As a role model for Chicanos, she had to chose carefully where and when to speak out.

In January of 1993, Cisneros received a letter from her friend Jasna in Sarajevo. The country of Yugoslavia was breaking apart. Jasna described conditions where Muslims, Croats, and Serbs battled one another. The fighting had destroyed entire villages. Many civilians had

In the Spotlight

Now, Cisneros was often invited to speak in Chicago. She had earned success, and she never forgot how hard she had to work. Cisneros told her audience, "Don't ever think writing is easy. My father couldn't understand that I could go to college and still not support myself. My mother, my six brothers had to support me. Making a living from writing is something new to me."[2]

Her unique style carried through to her appearance. One reporter wrote this description of her: "Cisneros has a voice like Tinker Bell's. . . . A tiny woman with cropped hair, she was wearing an ankle-length brown velvet dress and black suede boots and puffing on a cigar."[3]

Civilians and soldiers take cover behind a tank in Sarajevo in 1993. Cisneros spoke on behalf of her friend Jasna and the other innocents whose lives were torn apart by the war in Yugoslavia.

been killed or wounded. Bombs had destroyed houses and roads. Food and water were scarce. The city of Sarajevo was like a giant concentration camp.

Cisneros was distressed by the serious situation. But her friend was halfway around the world. What could one writer living in Texas do? For months, she was silent. She hoped others who had the means to help would step up. But nothing happened, and she felt powerless.

Finally, Cisneros realized that she had to speak out because she was different from others in San Antonio. She knew a real person living in Sarajevo. Her opportunity came at the city's International Women's Day Rally.

She spoke to the audience about Jasna's situation. She told them she had been waiting for world leaders to take action, but she now realized that "[w]e're world leaders, too. We don't think of that. Everybody that you come into contact with and everything that you do is going to have an effect. . . .[Y]ou can do something."[4]

Cisneros asked the American government to put an end to the fighting. She asked everyone in the audience to help in any way they could. "A woman is there. . . . Get her out. . . . Get them out. They're in that city, that country . . . that house on fire. . . . And I know that [woman]. . . . And I don't know what to do."[5] Her speech was later printed in the *New York Times*. By speaking out, Cisneros made a difference. She informed millions about the plight of her friend and others.

Until war ended in Sarajevo in 1996, Cisneros thought constantly about her friend. She prayed for the safety of Jasna and her family and sent them money. Cisneros was pleased that her reputation had given her the power to act. "There is so much that I can do as a writer to help meet my political aims. . . . I feel really blessed."[6]

Cisneros had three strikes against her when she decided to be a writer. She came from a lower-income family, she was a person of color, and she was a woman. But that did not keep her from becoming successful. Cisneros described authors with backgrounds like her own as "the illegal aliens of American lit" and "migrant workers in terms of respect."[7] In other words, she realized that writers of color had not been recognized by the American publishing industry or the literary field. Cisneros used her reputation to change that attitude.

In 1993, Cisneros was invited to give a reading at a Texas bookstore. She was interested until she learned that no other Latino had ever been invited to the store. She told the store owner that she would visit his store only if other Latino writers were invited.

Later that year, Cisneros was rewarded for her active support of other ethnic writers. She won the 1993 Anisfield-Wolf Book Award for *Woman Hollering Creek*. The award is given every year. It goes to writers whose work helps readers understand and appreciate other cultures.

The success of *The House on Mango Street* and *My Wicked Wicked Ways* was a track record that mainstream publishers understood. They realized that Cisneros was an author worth the risk of publishing. *Publishers Weekly* noted a trend in the 1990s. Latino writers moved from small presses to bigger houses. Cisneros was part of the publishing boom.

In 1994, Random House published three more of Cisneros's books. The first was a reprint of *The House on Mango Street* in English. In addition, a Spanish translation titled *La Casa en Mango Street* was released. Her third book was a picture book. *Hairs/Pelitos* was written for children ages four to eight. The text was a mix of Spanish and English. Cisneros shared her ideas of the similarities and differences among families of different backgrounds.

In 1995, the publisher Alfred A. Knopf reprinted *My*

Praise From Another Latino Writer

Gary Soto stated that Cisneros writes "in the show-me-don't-tell-me vein and her points leave valuable impressions. . . . [She also] incorporates Hispanic dialect, impressionistic metaphors, and social commentary in ways that reveal the fears and doubts unique to Hispanic women."[8]

Wicked Wicked Ways. Cisneros also continued to work with Turtle Bay Books. She knew that money earned from the sale of her books helped the publisher support unknown writers who were minorities.

By now, Cisneros had made a name for herself. She had earned the respect of the writing community. That same year, she received another important award. It came from the MacArthur Foundation. The foundation gives awards each year to talented individuals who have shown extraordinary originality and dedication in their creative pursuits. The fellowship came with a grant. Cisneros could use the money any way she pleased. This grant, her book royalties, and income from public speaking allowed her to live comfortable and write full-time. But, like Esperanza in *The House on Mango Street,* she would never forget her childhood growing up in the Chicago barrio.

A Mexican dancer entertains more than two hundred fans of *The House on Mango Street* during the 2009 Sandra Cisneros event at Norcross High School, celebrating the novel's twenty-fifth anniversary. More than two decades after its publication, the book continues to delight its readers.

11

Death and Change

With time and money to spare, Cisneros got started on another project. Her new idea grew from childhood stories. Bit by bit, she shared them with friends. She described the Cisneros family road trips. Her tales rolled on and on like the highways between Chicago and Mexico. Her story grew longer and bigger until Cisneros knew "it wasn't a short story, and [she] saved it for a novel."[1]

As she set to work on this novel, Cisneros compared her writing process to "cooking with intuition." The author explained that her mind "rummage[d] through its cupboards, then open[ed] the refrigerator in hopes of producing sweet and bittersweet courses."[2]

Her novel, titled *Caramelo,* was loosely based on her life and family. Cisneros often had to explain why it was fiction not fact. "Though the book was inspired by a real journey, I kept getting side tracked . . . the people are based on real people, but I invented things because I don't know what really happened." She also added a note at the front of the book. It says: "If, in the course of my inventing, I have inadvertently [accidentally] stumbled on the truth, *perdonenme* [pardon me]."[3]

The title of her new book was tied to her culture and her family history. Caramelo is a kind of Mexican candy. It also the word for a color that looks like burnt sugar. Cisneros's paternal grandmother had a *rebozo*, a shawl that color.

After Cisneros began work on *Caramelo,* a project she considered her father's story, Alfredo Cisneros had open-heart surgery. He came through the operation with no problems, but then his doctor diagnosed him with cancer. Cisneros knew her father would die before she completed his book. This was one of the saddest years of her life. Writing her father's story helped her deal with the loss. It helped her accept that her father was dying. She was able to "put all of that sadness in the book."[4]

Cisneros had a need to write *Caramelo.* She wanted to record her father's history as an American. Once her book was published, her father would not be forgotten. "I was trying to keep my father from fading," she said. "In Mexican culture we don't write things down."[5]

The money she had earned as a writer also allowed her another "great, lasting gift."[6] She put her writing on hold in 1995. She spent the last year her father had left with him in Chicago. Alfredo Cisneros died on February 12, 1997. For some time, Cisneros could not write. Many months passed before she went back to work on his story, *Caramelo*.

In 1997, Cisneros, age forty-two, found a colorful way to make the news. She painted her home in San Antonio bright purple. Her Victorian cottage was located in the King William neighborhood, a historic district. The city's design and review commission had to approve paint colors used on houses in that area. It was the commission's job to make sure the area looked much as it did when it was first developed.

Cisneros felt her color choice fit well with the city's Mexican heritage. The land where her home sat had once been part of Mexico. Bright colors such as purple, green, red, orange, and pink are typically used in Mexico. Her choice of color celebrated the rich history of San Antonio that was entwined with Mexico.

The board did not agree. They ruled that the color was "historically inappropriate." For the next two years, the disagreement was in the news. It also made the front page of the *New York Times*.

Cisneros researched the issue. She submitted a paper to the board. She found that no records had been kept about colors of paint used in the poorer Mexican neighborhoods of the city. Records were kept only for wealthier areas. Cisneros considered this racism, saying: "We are a people *sin papeles* (without papers)! We don't exist."[7]

Her neighbors were also divided over the dispute. Some agreed with Cisneros. They backed her claim

Trolley Tours

During the debate over her house, Sandra Cisneros's purple home became a popular stop on the sightseeing trolley tours. Many neighbors who did not like Cisneros's choice of color also did not like trolleys driving by. Cisneros added fuel to the fire when she posted a sign in her yard reading: "We Love Trolleys."

of racism. Others did not like the purple house. They thought Cisneros was looking for ways to get more publicity.

After two years, Cisneros and the commission reached a compromise. The commission waived the fines that could run as high as one thousand dollars each day. Cisneros agreed to paint her house pink. But she did not change the color immediately so that was not the end of the matter.

A few months later, Cisneros gave the commission a sample of the paint from her house. The color had faded after two years in the sun. The commission ruled that the color had faded to violet. That color was acceptable.

Cisneros joked about the situation, saying, "I don't know why some paint company hasn't snatched me up to be spokeswoman for their new *Tejano* palette!"[8] She also suggested that she might write a book about her colorful controversy. She said it would be a coloring book.

Her purple paint continued to fade. After a few more years in the Texas sun, it was blue. Then Cisneros had the house painted bright Mexican pink. She also built an office in the backyard. She had that building painted Mexican marigold. "The colors make me happy," she said.[9]

Cisneros's battle over her colorful home drew attention to the Chicano community in San Antonio. It also earned the author a reputation for doing as she pleased.

Cisneros often returned to Chicago to visit her family. She also stayed involved with the city's Latino

Sandra Cisneros's controversial purple house with the "We Love Trolleys" sign.

Strong Chicano Supporter

Regardless of what others thought, Cisneros stood firm on her beliefs. The *Texas Monthly Magazine* had asked to interview her in 1995. Cisneros agreed to be interviewed but only by a Latino author. The magazine refused.

When *Texas Monthly* asked to interview her about the dispute over her purple house, she again refused, explaining that she could not cooperate "with a magazine that printed so few works by Hispanic writers."[10]

community, lending support to programs that encourage self-esteem and pride in young people.

One program she favored was the Chernin Center for the Arts. When it opened on November 19, 1997, the new Chernin Center became the only Chicago YMCA dedicated to the arts. The center was near three Chicago barrios and the University of Illinois. The center offered programs such as tennis and basketball, but it focused mainly on the arts. Chernin's executive director said that the arts and communication programs helped "to build self-esteem and pride in our young people."[11] Cisneros agreed and was glad to help.

In 1998, Chicago's Mexican Fine Arts Center Museum honored Cisneros. The ceremony was held during the Sor Juana Festival, honoring seventeenth-century Mexican poet Sor Juana Inés de la Cruz. She was a great lyric poet of the colonial era. The annual festival includes an exhibit of Mexican and Mexican-American arts. Each year, the museum honors five outstanding women. The award recognizes work that influences the city of Chicago in a positive way.

Cisneros continued to share her time and energy by helping other writers, students, and adults. She talked to writers' groups and to students. She received many invitations but could only accept a few. Cisneros agreed to visit Greg Mitchie's classroom. He was a teacher in Chicago. As she toured his classroom, she was impressed with his passion for art, music, and drama. What impressed her even more was his sincere interest in his barrio students and their culture.

Mitchie later wrote a book about his teaching experiences in Chicago's secondary schools titled: *Holler If You Hear Me: The Education of a Teacher and His Students.* Cisneros wrote the foreword for the book.

In the foreword, Cisneros recalls meeting some of Mitchie's students four years after her visit to his classroom. They all attended a reading Cisneros gave at Chicago's Mexican Fine Arts Center. The students were then in college. In the book, Cisneros gave their enthusiastic teacher credit for their success. She ended her comments with this thought: "It is a great and marvelous thing to be reminded that to change the world we need only to change ourselves. Greg Mitchie and his students give me that hope."[12]

Cisneros continued to speak out on issues from presidential candidates to capital punishment. In 1998, George W. Bush of Texas decided to run for president of the United States. One reporter quoted the San Antonio

Education and People of Color Now

Cisneros feels that schools still do not provide for the needs of minority students. As a group, they are often overlooked and ignored. In her opinion, many people who live in this country treat all people of color the same way. "[There is] so little that mainstream America knows about us," the author once stated.[13]

Cisneros also objects to the way Latinos are often portrayed in books and stories that students read or in television programs and movies that people watch. Their characters are stereotyped. They do not represent what life is really like growing up poor or as a person of color in America. Most important, they often do not show Latinos as hard-working, intelligent, and creative people.

author after she said, "[S]ome Hispanics are charmed by the governor's Spanish speaking."[14]

Her statement was reprinted by the *Chicago Tribune*, leaving the impression that Cisneros endorsed Bush. The *Chicago Tribune* quickly had to print a retraction. The paper informed readers that part of Cisneros's comments had been omitted. She had also said "that for Bush to confront the many serious issues concerning Hispanics, [he was] going to need a lot more than '*como esta usted?* [How are you?]'"[15] Her full statement suggested that she did not support Bush and felt that the candidate had little understanding of Latinos.

Cisneros also worked to put an end to the death

penalty. In November 2000, she and several other writers petitioned President Bill Clinton to take action. The letter addressed the plight of one federal prisoner, Juan Raul Garza, who had been convicted of murder. He was to be executed on December 12.

The letter reminded President Clinton that almost 75 percent of prisoners executed by the federal government are people of color. This high percentage indicates that something may be wrong with the court sentencing system. The group also expressed the concern that Garza's sentence was stiffer because of his skin color than that of a white prisoner who had committed the same crime. The group asked that Garza's sentence be changed to life in prison without possibility for release. President Clinton postponed the execution and agreed to study the case. But Garza was executed the following June.

However, the writers' protests against the death penalty, along with those of may other people, did have an effect. Texas had 450 prisons on death row at the end of 2000. Only the state of California had more prisoners awaiting execution. Now, the state of Texas is investigating many cases of prisoners on death row to be certain that they were treated fairly.

Sandra Cisneros also honored her father's memory in 2000 with the creation of the Alfredo Cisneros Del Moral Foundation. "My father lived his life as an example of generosity and honest labor," Cisneros wrote. "He would sooner rip the seams of a cushion apart and do it over than put his name on an item that wasn't up to his high standards. I especially wanted to . . . showcase writers who are equally proud of their own craft."[16] Writers must be nominated for this award. The recipients need to demonstrate exceptional talent and a sincere commitment to their form of expression.

The House on Mango Street was now an audiobook. Cisneros was the reader. It was a perfect fit. According to one reviewer: "[H]er pitch is perfect, her rhythm is rollicking, and the language is always refreshingly honest and wise."[17] One of Cisneros's short stories was included in a collection titled *Short Fiction on Faith*. It was published by Beacon Press. She continued to work on her novel *Caramelo*. The successful author was now much in demand. She began to do public readings from the draft in 2002. Her audience liked what they heard. Many considered it Cisneros's best work so far. They thought *Caramelo* would bring the Latina author even more fame. She was asked to read and lecture in many places across the country. Cisneros discovered that "it was hard to be withdrawn and be quiet and work on the book."[18]

12

Writing All Alone in Her Pajamas

Caramelo was published on September 24, 2002. The forty-seven-year-old author took nine years to complete her novel. Cisneros recalled that she originally set out to write a short story. But *Caramelo* ended up as a 450-page family saga. The author enjoyed the time spent with her characters. By the end of the final chapter, she knew them well.

Cisneros is often asked how it felt to work on one story for so long. "For me it didn't seem like it was that long," she said. "[I] put my head down for a few seconds and then when I looked up nine years had passed. . . . I work very slowly, so sometimes I lose touch with reality."[1] Working on her family saga was a struggle. Cisneros often got so involved in her book, that she did not leave her house for days. She experienced what she called "writer's terror."[2] "There were times . . . that I really was lost," she said. "In the fifth year and sixth year I was in deep despair. I was very blocked and frightened by the deadline and the enormity of what I had created. I was just trying to tell a simple tale and it had just gotten out of hand."[3]

A friend told her that she needed to get out of the house and have some fun. Cisneros listened to this advice. It helped her get beyond her "terrors" and continue with her writing.

Caramelo is the story of a family car trip from Chicago to Mexico. The narrator is Celaya "Lala" Reyes, a young Mexican-American girl. The book builds on many of the ideas and issues Cisneros explored in *The House on Mango Street.*

In this novel, Cisneros added another layer. *Caramelo* is also a history. It tells about relations between Mexico and the United States. It looks at how the cultures of both countries shaped the life of the Reyes family. The story tells of one family's trip, but it describes the experiences of many families. Cisneros's new novel incorporates more than just aspects of her father's story, it also tells the tale of all Mexican Americans who move back and forth across the border.

The novel is based in part on Cisneros's childhood memories, but she tells readers that her book is "nothing but story, bits of string, odds and ends found here and there, embroidered together to make something new."[4] She said she wrote this book to learn more about herself. She explored the borders of her life. She is fascinated by the boundaries that divide countries and cultures.

As she wrote *Caramelo,* Cisneros traveled back and forth between the borders of "truth, fiction and the place they mix." She hopes her story will lead "readers . . . into unfamiliar territory."[5]

Random House released two editions of *Caramelo.* One hundred thirty-five thousand copies were printed in English. Another twenty-three thousand copies were printed in Spanish. The release of such a huge number of books was unusual. It showed that Random House had faith in its Latino author. They expected Cisneros's new book to be a best seller.

To help sell all those copies, Cisneros traveled across the United States. She gave readings and signed books. She also toured Spain and Mexico. This was another first for Cisneros. Her novel was the first book written by a Latino from the United States to receive so much publicity in Spanish-speaking countries.

Critics praised *Caramelo.* Reviewer Margaret Randall said that "Cisneros's unique use of language lift[ed] *Caramelo* from the category of a very fine novel and [placed] it among the great literatures of our time."[6]

Cisneros was also pleased with her work. She knew that her writing style had grown and matured. She said, "You can see how I have taken everything that I have learned and 20 years later, here is a writer who has learned to write fiction."[7]

For the next three years, Cisneros continued to write and also to teach workshops around her kitchen table. With each new project, she grew as a writer, saying

"I try to do what's hard for me, what I haven't done in the past."[8] Her stories and poems were published in several anthologies. Her list of books sold well, and in 2005, *Loose Woman* and *Woman Hollering Creek* were released as Books on Tape.

In 2006, Cisneros created another gift for the writers' community, the Macondo Foundation. The concept grew from writing workshops first held in Cisneros's kitchen. She started with fifteen students, but that number quickly grew to more than one hundred participants.

The Macondo Foundation brings a diversity of writers together, crossing borders of all kinds. Its goal is to unite writers and to advance creativity, to foster generosity, and to honor community. Each year during the last week of July, literary and musical events are held in San Antonio, Texas, to raise money to support the foundation's residency program for writers and other projects.

More than thirty years ago, Sandra Cisneros dreamed of a career as a writer. Today, her dream has come true. She took her first steps along the path while a student at the Iowa Writers' Workshop. It was a difficult time for Cisneros. She felt out of place. She questioned who she was and what she had to say. Then she realized something important. Cisneros realized that she was unique. She decided to write about subjects that her classmates knew nothing about. She discovered her own writing style. She found her voice.

Cisneros is a mainstream author with many "firsts" on her list of achievements. She was the first Chicana

Sandra Cisneros's unique voice has reached beyond the literary world. Mexico's first lady at the time, Martha Sahagun (left), and the then first lady of the United States, Laura Bush (center), stand with artists Angel Rodriguez-Diaz and Maricela Sanchez in 2001. Behind them is a portrait Rodriguez-Diaz painted of Sandra Cisneros titled "The Protagonist of an Endless Story."

to be published by a major publishing house. The advance she received was the largest ever made to a Mexican-American writer. She continued to work hard at her career and made a name for herself. This success brought her another reward. She was the first Chicana to support herself with her writing.

Success has given her a strong voice. Cisneros decided to use her writing and voice to speak out for other Latinos. She supports women's movements, focusing her

Viva Success!

More than twenty-five years after it was first published, *The House on Mango Street* is a classic. The book is assigned reading for university students at Yale and Stanford. The novel is listed on many required reading lists for high-school students.

More than two million copies of the English version of *The House on Mango Street* have been sold since it was published by Vintage in 1991. In addition, the Spanish version, *La Casa en Mango Street*, has also sold more than ninety-five thousand copies in the United States and Puerto Rico.

In 2001, Cisneros's hometown honored *The House on Mango Street*. It was one of the titles considered for the "One Book, One Chicago" project. The citywide reading program is sponsored by the public library.

concerns on helping women of color. In her role as a spokesperson, she is not shy. Cisneros says, "I am taking my lumps and bumps for being a big mouth . . . but usually from those whose opinion I don't respect." She adds, "I try to be as honest about what I see and to speak rather than be silent, especially if it means I can save lives, or serve humanity."[9]

Cisneros has given the Latino community another gift—her example. She lives with her two cultures. She defied Mexican-American stereotypes and became a role model. She chose to be independent. She challenged herself to learn and grow. In doing so, Cisneros became like the characters in her stories. She is passionate and powerful. She can be tender and hot tempered. She is brave and above all, she is a fierce woman, one who has earned respect.

Cisneros often talks to young writers. She offers them sound advice. She knows how badly they want to be published. Her advice, though, is to "be in a hurry to become a good writer."[10] She assures them that getting published will take care of itself.

She also tells them to have another career—a job that provides a steady income. Young writers must assume they will "never make any money from . . . writing."[11] But they should not to be concerned by that. She adds, "Making money isn't a measure of the worth of your writing."[12]

Sometimes, she gives them assignments. One of her favorites is to have students make lists. She asks them to list ten things that make them different from anyone in the room, in their community, in the United Sates, or in their family.

She also shares tips to get beyond writer's block. When one is stuck, she says "leave the room and go to an art exhibit. Change the subject because if you get off the track, you will get *on* the track. . . . If it's not working today, I put it away. It'll [the writing] find its time."[13]

Cisneros also talks about how she collects words, expressions, and Spanish rhythms to use in her writing. She fills files with dialogue and conversations she overhears and suggests other writers do the same. Cisneros goes on to explain how she uses these word files to suit her own purpose. She mixes and matches the bits of conversation because "real life doesn't have a shape. You have to snip and cut."[14]

Her word files were very helpful as she wrote *Woman Hollering Creek*. The collection of stories had many different characters. And each one needed to speak with a unique voice.

Another resource Cisneros uses is the San Antonio phone book. For her it's a great resource to find just the right name for a character. First, she scans the pages for a last name that she likes. Then she looks for a first name. If she needs the name of a store or business, Cisneros reads through the Yellow Pages and mail-order catalogues to look for ideas.

Cisneros looks forward to new writing challenges. Unfortunately, she will not share future successes with the

Latino Writing

Cisneros also saw a bright future for other writers. "Chicano writers have a lot to say. The influence of our two languages is profound."[15]

"Now when I see my name in print and my name on the side of the book, that makes me so happy. I'm the one who put it there. I just feel so proud of myself."[16] But she believes the best work of her career is yet to come. In her opinion, the female writers she has read reached their peaks when they were in their sixties. "It's a wonderful profession when you can look forward to your 60s."[17]

Sandra Cisneros lectures at Cornell University on September 13, 2007, as part of the Creative Writing Reading series, inspiring the next generation of authors.

woman who encouraged her over the years. Her mother, Elvira Cisneros, passed away on November 1, 2007. She was seventy-eight years old. Her daughter mourned the loss of her mother and in her honor established the Elvira Cordero Cisneros Award. Recipients are selected for exhibiting exceptional talent and a dedication to the work of nurturing the creativity of others. Cisneros explains, "We wanted to give it [the award] to someone who is too busy nurturing others to nurture herself. My mother was a deeply creative, but frustrated artist, and I don't want to see others live their lives with regrets for what they didn't do."[18]

Today, Cisneros divides her time between speaking engagements and new writing challenges. She is working on several projects including "stories, poems, children's books, essays and a collection of short, short, short fiction" titled *Infinito*.[19] Cisneros also serves as writer-in-residence at Our Lady of the Lake University in San Antonio. She works hard to balance public time and her private life. She needs solitude to write and often works in her pajamas.

Sandra Cisneros still calls San Antonio home. She lives in her bright Mexican-pink house with many creatures "little and large," happily single, and in love with life.

Chronology

1954—Sandra Cisneros is born on December 20 in Chicago, Illinois.

1959—Begins school.

1966—Family buys first house, a bungalow in a poor neighborhood in south Chicago, and moves in.

1968—Attends Josephinum Academy, an all-girls Catholic high school.

1972—Graduates from high school; attends Loyola College, Chicago, Illinois.

1976—Graduates from Loyola College; enters University of Iowa Writers' Workshop.

1978—Receives Master's of Fine Arts degree from University of Iowa; begins writing stories for *The House on Mango Street*.

1979–1981—Works at Latino Youth Alternative High School in Chicago counseling students; poetry included in Chicago Transit Authority's poetry project.

1980–1981—Works for Loyola University recruiting students; Cisneros's first collection of poems, *Bad Boys*, is published.

1982–1983—Receives first NEA grant; leaves Chicago for Massachusetts and works to complete *The House on Mango Street*; travels to Europe, serves as artist-in-residence at Michael Karolyi Foundation in Venice, Italy; meets lifelong friend Jasna in Sarajevo, Yugoslavia.

1984—*The House on Mango Street* is published to positive reviews; Cisneros takes a job at Guadalupe Cultural Arts Center in San Antonio, Texas.

1985—Receives the Before Columbus Foundation's American Book Award for *The House on Mango Street*; receives Dobie Paisano Fellowship.

1987—*My Wicked Wicked Ways* published; takes position as visiting professor at California State University, Chico; receives second NEA grant; contacts literary agent Susan Bergholz; *The House on Mango Street* and *Woman Hollering Creek* sold to Random House/Vintage Press.

1991—*Woman Hollering Creek* published by Random House; Cisneros receives Lannan Literary Award; Vintage Books reprints *The House on Mango Street*.

1992—Receives advance from Random House for new novel, *Caramelo*, and another for collection of poems, *Loose Woman*; Turtle Bay Books reprints *My Wicked Wicked Ways*.

1993—Becomes activist to help Jasna; *Woman Hollering Creek* wins the Anisfield-Wolf Award for excellence in literature of diversity.

1994—Turtle Bay Books publishes *Loose Woman*; Knopf publishes *Hairs/Pelitos*, a children's book; Random House publishes *La Casa en Mango Street*, the Spanish version of her first novel.

1995—Receives a MacArthur Fellowship.

1997—Father, Alfredo Cisneros dies on February 12; Cisneros paints San Antonio home purple and creates controversy.

1998—Honored with a lifetime achievement award from the Mexican Fine Arts Center Museum, Chicago; audio version of *The House on Mango Street* released with Cisneros as reader.

2000—Voices her support to end capital punishment.

2001—*The House on Mango Street* is considered for Chicago's "One Book, One Chicago" project.

2002—Cisneros gives public readings from new novel, *Caramelo*; Knopf publishes *Caramelo* in English and Spanish; Cisneros tours in the United States, Spain, and Mexico

2003—Cisneros continues to write and teach workshops; selected works published in two anthologies: *Writing on the Edge: A Borderlands Reader*, edited by Tom Miller, University of Arizona Press, and *Lone Star Literature: From the Red River to the Rio Grande*, edited by Don Graham, W. W. Norton & Company; *Caramelo* reprint edition released by Vintage Press in September.

2004–2005—*Loose Woman* and *Woman Hollering Creek* released by Books on Tape.

2006—Cisneros officially incorporated the Macondo Foundation, an organization committed to bringing together a diversity of writers crossing borders of all kinds.

2007—Mother, Elvira Cisneros, dies on November 1; Cisneros takes leave from her writing to mourn her death.

2008—Cisneros resumes her work in July at her annual workshop called Macondo; she lives in San Antonio and continues to write, lecture, travel, and actively support political issues.

Chapter Notes

CHAPTER 1. THE HOUSE ON MANGO STREET

1. Sandra Cisneros, *The House on Mango Street* (New York: Alfred A. Knopf, 1994), xxi.
2. Ibid., xiii.
3. Jim Sagel, "Sandra Cisneros: Conveying the Riches of the Latin American Culture Is the Author's Literary Goal," *Publisher's Weekly*, March 29, 1991, *Las Mujeres*, 2007, <http://www.lasmujeres.com/en/?m=sandra-cisneros&s=articles&sc=art_conveying-the-riches> (August 15, 2007).
4. Ibid.
5. Ibid.
6. Ibid.
7. Cisneros, xvi.
8. Ibid., xvii.
9. Ibid., p. 4.
10. Ibid., p. 105.
11. Ana Caban, "'Mango Street' Ripens Into Lyrical Literary Success," *Milwaukee Journal-Sentinel*, October 12, 2003, <http://www.jsonline.com/story/index.aspx?id=176182> (August 3, 2007).
12. Ibid.
13. Sandra Cisneros, "Sandra Cisneros," *SandraCisneros.com*, n.d., <http://www.sandracisneros.com> (August 3, 2007).
14. "A Conversation With Sandra Cisneros," *Miambiance*, January 1, 2003, <http://www.mdc.edu/kendall/miambiancemagazine/issue13/interview.html> (August 3, 2007).

15. Ron Charles, "Threads of a Colorful Family," *Christian Science Monitor*, Vol. 94, No. 223, October 10, 2002, p. 19.
16. Caban.

CHAPTER 2. IN THE BARRIO

1. Sandra Cisneros, "Border Crossings and Beyond," *Studies in Short Fiction*, Summer 1994, Vol. 31, No. 3, pp. 415–424, Literature of the American Minorities class Web site, Edgwood College Department of English, April 25, 2000, <http://english.edgewood.edu/eng242/Sandra_Cisneros_Border_Crossings_and_beyond.htm> (August 17, 2007).
2. Ibid.
3. Pilar E. Rodriguez Aranda, "On the Solitary Fate of Being Mexican, Female, Wicked and Thirty-three: An Interview With Writer Sandra Cisneros," *Americas Review*, Vol. 18, Spring 1990, pp. 64–80.
4. "Sandra Cisneros," *Major Authors and Illustrators for Children and Young Adults*, 2nd ed., 8 vols., Gale Group, 2002, reproduced in *Biography Resource Center* (Farmington Hills, Mich.: Thomson Gale, 2007), <http://www.edupaperback.org/showauth.cfm?authid=259> (October 25, 2007).
5. Jim Sagel, "Sandra Cisneros: Conveying the Riches of the Latin American Culture Is the Author's Literary Goal," *Publisher's Weekly*, March 29, 1991, *Las Mujeres*, 2007, <http://www.lasmujeres.com/en/?m=sandra-cisneros&s=articles&sc=art_conveying-the-riches> (August 15, 2007).
6. Sandra Cisneros, "Only Daughter," *Glamour*, November 1990, pp. 256–258.
7. Ibid.
8. "Hispanic Heritage: Biographies: Sandra Cisneros," *Gale Cengage Learning*, n.d., <http://www.galegroup.com/

free_resources/chh/bio/cisneros_s.htm> (August 13, 2007).

9. "Sandra Cisneros Quotes," *Brainy Quotes*, 2008, <http://www.brainyquote.com/quotes/authors/s/ sandra_cisneros.html> (August 15, 2007).

10. Cisneros, "Only Daughter," pp. 256–258.

11. Cisneros, "Border Crossings and Beyond."

12. Gregg Barrios, "The Nature of Sandra Cisneros," *Nature Conservancy Magazine*, September 1, 2003, <http://www.nature.org/magazine/fall2003/friends/index.html> (August 3, 2007).

13. Sandra Cisneros, "Border Crossings and Beyond."

14. Ibid.

CHAPTER 3. A HOUSE, NOT A HOME

1. Melita Marie Garza, "Author Sandra Cisneros Tells Her Story to Latino Schoolchildren," *Seattle Times*, December 28, 1992, <http://community.seattletimes.nwsource.com/ archive/?date=19921228&slug=1532440> (October 30, 2007).

2. Sandra Cisneros, "Ghosts and Voices, Writing From Obsession," *Americas Review*, Vol. 15, No. 1, Spring 1987, p. 71.

3. Sandra Cisneros, "Border Crossings and Beyond," *Studies in Short Fiction*, Summer 1994, Vol. 31, No. 3, pp. 415–424, Literature of the American Minorities class Web site, Edgwood College Department of English, April 25, 2000, <http://english.edgewood.edu/eng242/Sandra_Cisneros_Border_Crossings_and_beyond.htm> (August 17, 2007).

4. "Hispanic Heritage: Biographies: Sandra Cisneros," *Gale Cengage Learning*, n.d., <http://www.galegroup.com/free_resources/chh/bio/cisneros_s.htm> (August 13, 2007).

5. Ibid.
6. "Sandra Cisneros," *Major Authors and Illustrators for Children and Young Adults*, 2nd ed., 8 vols., Gale Group, 2002, reproduced in *Biography Resource Center* (Farmington Hills, Mich.: Thomson Gale, 2007), <http:// www.edupaperback.org/showauth.cfm?authid=259> (October 25, 2007).
7. Ibid.
8. Ibid.
9. "Sandra Cisneros," *Contemporary Hispanic Biography*, Vol. 1, Gale Group, 2002, *Embassy of the United States Dar Es Salaam, Tanzania*, n.d., <http://Tanzania.usembassy. gov/hhm-sandracisneros.html> (October 10, 2007).
10. Cisneros, "Border Crossings and Beyond."
11. "A Conversation With Sandra Cisneros," *Miambiance*, January 1, 2003, <http://www.mdc.edu/kendall/ miambiancemagazine/issue13/interview.html> (August 3, 2007).

CHAPTER 4. A YOUNG WRITER

1. "Sandra Cisneros," *Major Authors and Illustrators for Children and Young Adults*, 2nd ed., 8 vols., Gale Group, 2002, reproduced in *Biography Resource Center* (Farmington Hills, Mich.: Thomson Gale, 2007), <http:// www.edupaperback.org/showauth.cfm?authid=259> (October 25, 2007).
2. Ibid.
3. Ibid.
4. Gregg Barrios, "The Nature of Sandra Cisneros," *Nature Conservancy Magazine*, September 1, 2003,<http://www. nature.org/magazine/fall2003/friends/index.html> (August 3, 2007).
5. Sandra Cisneros, "Notes to a Young(er) Writer," *Americas Review*, Vol. 15, Spring 1987, pp. 74–76.

6. Ibid.
7. Sandra Cisneros, "Border Crossings and Beyond," *Studies in Short Fiction*, Summer 1994, Vol. 31, No. 3, pp. 415–424, Literature of the American Minorities class Web site, Edgwood College Department of English, April 25, 2000, <http://english.edgewood.edu/eng242/Sandra_Cisneros_Border_Crossings_and_beyond.htm> (August 17, 2007).

CHAPTER 5. A "WACKY" VOICE ALL HER OWN

1. "Sandra Cisneros," *Contemporary Hispanic Biography*, Vol. 1, Gale Group, 2002, *Embassy of the United States Dar Es Salaam, Tanzania*, n.d., <http://Tanzania.usembassy.gov/hhm-sandracisneros.html> (October 10, 2007).
2. Ibid.
3. Sandra Cisneros, "Notes to a Young(er) Writer," *Americas Review*, Vol. 15, Spring 1987, pp. 71–76.
4. Ibid.
5. "Sandra Cisneros," *Major Authors and Illustrators for Children and Young Adults*, 2nd ed., 8 vols., Gale Group, 2002, reproduced in *Biography Resource Center* (Farmington Hills, Mich.: Thomson Gale, 2007), <http://www.edupaperback.org/showauth.cfm?authid=259> (October 25, 2007).
6. Ibid.
7. Ibid.
8. Ibid.

CHAPTER 6. STORIES OR "HEALTHY LIES"

1. Sandra Cisneros, *The House on Mango Street* (New York: Alfred A. Knopf, 1994), xvii.

2. Gregory Michie, *Holler If You Hear Me: The Education of a Teacher and His Students* (New York: Teachers College Press, 1999), ix.

3. Ibid., xi.

4. Renee H. Shea, "Truth, Lies, and Memory: A Profile of Sandra Cisneros," *Poets & Writers*, September/October 2002, p. 32.

5. Sandra Cisneros, "Notes to a Young(er) Writer," *Americas Review*, Vol. 15, Spring 1987, pp. 74–76.

6. Feroza Jussawalla and Reed Way Dasenbrock, *Interview With Writers of the Post-Colonial World* (Jackson, Miss.: University Press of Mississippi, 1992), p. 290.

7. Sandra Cisneros, "Do You Know Me? I Wrote *The House on Mango Street*," *Americas Review*, Vol. 15, No. 1, Spring 1987, pp. 78–79.

8. Pilar E. Rodriguez Aranda, "On the Solitary Fate of Being Mexican, Female, Wicked and Thirty-three: An Interview With Writer Sandra Cisneros," *Americas Review*, Vol. 18, Spring 1990, p. 69.

9. Ibid.

CHAPTER 7. CHICANA AROUND THE WORLD

1. Feroza Jussawalla and Reed Way Dasenbrock, *Interviews With Writers of the Post-Colonial World* (Jackson, Miss.: University Press of Mississippi, 1992), p. 298.

2. Sandra Cisneros, "Do You Know Me? I Wrote *The House on Mango Street*," *Americas Review*, Vol. 15, No. 1, Spring 1987, p. 79.

3. Ibid.

4. Gwendolyn Brooks, review of *The House on Mango Street*, by Sandra Cisneros, *Amazon.com*, n.d., <http://www.amazon.com/House-Mango-Street-Sandra-

Cisneros/dp/product-description/0679734775>
(October 16, 2008).

5. Ibid.
6. Ibid.
7. Adult Fiction Reviews, *The House on Mango Street*, by Sandra Cisneros, *Booklist*, October 15, 1984, p. 28.
8. Gary Soto, "Voices of Sadness and Science," *Bloomsbury Review*, July/August 1988, p. 21.

CHAPTER 8. TEJANOS AND TEXAS

1. Gregg Barrios, "The Nature of Sandra Cisneros," *Nature Conservancy Magazine*, September 1, 2003, <http://www.nature.org/magazine/fall2003/friends/index.html> (August 3, 2007).
2. Virginia Brackett, *A Home in the Heart: The Story of Sandra Cisneros* (Greensboro, N.C.: Morgan Reynolds Publishing, Inc., 2005), p. 54.
3. Feroza Jussawalla and Reed Way Dasenbrock, *Interviews With Writers of the Post-Colonial World* (Jackson, Miss.: University Press of Mississippi, 1992), p. 299.
4. Ibid.
5. Pilar E. Rodriguez Aranda, "On the Solitary Fate of Being Mexican, Female, Wicked and Thirty-three: An Interview With Writer Sandra Cisneros," *Americas Review*, Vol. 18, Spring 1990, p. 70.
6. Jussawalla and Dasenbrock, p. 291.
7. Sandra Cisneros, "Ghosts and Voices: Writing From Obsession," *Americas Review*, vol. 15, No. 1, Spring 1987, p. 61.
8. Ibid., p. 73.
9. "A Conversation With Sandra Cisneros," *Miambiance*, January 1, 2003, <http://www.mdc.edu/kendall/miambiancemagazine/issue13/interview.html> (August 3, 2007).

10. Cisneros, "Ghosts and Voices," p. 73.
11. Sandra Cisneros, *The House on Mango Street* (New York: Alfred A. Knopf, 1994), p. 75.
12. Ibid.
13. Sandra Cisneros, "Notes to a Young(er) Writer," *Americas Review*, Vol. 15, Spring 1987, p. 74.
14. Ibid., p. 76.

CHAPTER 9. TIME TO WRITE

1. Robert Birnbaum, "Sandra Cisneros: Author of *Caramelo* Talks With Robert Birnbaum." *Identity Theory*, December 4, 2002.
2. Virginia Brackett, *A Home in the Heart: The Story of Sandra Cisneros* (Greensboro, N.C.: Morgan Reynolds Publishing, Inc., 2005), p. 62.
3. Melita Marie Garza, "Author Sandra Cisneros Tells Her Story to Latino Schoolchildren," *Seattle Times*, December 28, 1992, <http://community.seattletimes. nwsource.com/archive/?date=19921228&slug= 1532440> (October 30, 2007).
4. Jim Sagel, "Sandra Cisneros: Conveying the Riches of the Latin American Culture Is the Author's Literary Goal," *Publisher's Weekly*, March 29, 1991, *Las Mujeres*, 2007, <http://www.lasmujeres.com/en/?m=sandra-cisneros&s=articles&sc=art_conveying-the-riches> (August 15, 2007).
5. Sandra Cisneros, "Notes to a Young(er) Writer," *Americas Review*, Vol. 15, Spring 1987, p. 76.
6. Garza.
7. Brackett, p. 67.
8. Dan Schneider, "This Old Poem #23," *Cosmoetica*, September 15, 2002, <http://www.cosmoetica.com/ TOP23-DES21.htm> (August 15, 2007).

9. Pilar E. Rodriguez Aranda, "On the Solitary Fate of Being Mexican, Female, Wicked and Thirty-three: An Interview With Writer Sandra Cisneros," *Americas Review*, Vol. 18, Spring 1990, p. 75.

10. Ibid., p. 76.

11. Garza.

12. Sandra Cisneros, "Border Crossings and Beyond," *Studies in Short Fiction*, Summer 1994, Vol. 31, No. 3, pp. 415–424, Literature of the American Minorities class Web site, Edgwood College Department of English, April 25, 2000, <http://english.edgewood.edu/eng242/ Sandra_Cisneros_ Border_Crossings_and_beyond.htm> (August 17, 2007).

13. Gregg Barrios, "The Nature of Sandra Cisneros," *Nature Conservancy Magazine*, September 1, 2003, <http://www. nature.org/magazine/fall2003/friends/index.html> (August 3, 2007).

CHAPTER 10. SPEAKING OUT

1. Pilar E. Rodriguez Aranda, "On the Solitary Fate of Being Mexican, Female, Wicked and Thirty-three: An Interview With Writer Sandra Cisneros," *Americas Review*, Vol. 18, Spring 1990, p. 66.

2. Ibid.

3. Melita Marie Garza, "Author Sandra Cisneros Tells Her Story to Latino Schoolchildren," *Seattle Times*, December 28, 1992, <http://community.seattletimes. nwsource.com/ archive/?date=19921228&slug= 1532440> (October 30, 2007).

4. Ibid.

5. Sandra Cisneros, "Who Wants Stories Now?" *New York Times*, April 14, 1993, section. 4, p. 17.

6. "Sandra Cisneros," *Major Authors and Illustrators for Children and Young Adults*, 2nd ed., 8 vols., Gale Group, 2002, reproduced in *Biography Resource Center*

(Farmington Hills, Mich.: Thomson Gale, 2007), <http://www.edupaperback.org/showauth.cfm?authid=259> (October 25, 2007).

7. Ibid.

8. *UXL World Encyclopedia of World Biography*, s.v. "Sandra Cisneros," *FindArticles.com*, October 15, 2008, <http://findarticles.com/p/articles/mi_gx5229/is_2003/ai_n19145663> (October, 25, 2007).

Chapter 11. Death and Change

1. Heidi Benson, "Author Traces the Many Paths of Her Father's Story," *San Francisco Chronicle*, October 25, 2002, <http://www.sfgate.com/cgi-bin/article.cgi?f=/c/a/2002/10/25/DD36246.DTL&hw=heidi+benson+author+traces+the+many&sn=005&sc=262> (October 15, 2008).

2. Diane Urbani, "Cisneros Takes Adoring Audience for Ride," *Deseret Morning News*, September 21, 2003, *FindArticles.com*, October 15, 2008, <http://findarticles.com/p/articles/mi_qn4188/is_20030921/ai_n11416161> (October 15, 2008).

3. Benson.

4. Jen Buckendorff, "Father's Death Opened New Insights for 'Caramelo' Author Sandra Cisneros," *Seattle Times*, October 21, 2003.

5. Adriana Lopez, "Caramel-Colored Prose," *Library Journal*, September 15, 2002, <http://www.libraryjournal.com/article/CA242273.html> (October 15, 2008).

6. Benson.

7. Kathy Lowry, "The Purple Passion of Sandra Cisneros," *Texas Monthly*, October 1997, p. 149.

8. Ibid., p. 150.

9. Sandra Cisneros, "About Sandra Cisneros," *SandraCisneros.com*, June 4, 2008, <http://www.sandracisneros.com/bio.php> (October 15, 2008).

10. Lowry, p. 150.

11. Rohan B. Preston, "New YMCA Center Backs Arts," *Chicago Tribune*, November 19, 1997, Metro Section, p. 3.

12. Gregory Mitchie, *Holler If You Hear Me: The Education of a Teacher and His Students* (New York: Teachers College Press, 1999), x.

13. "Sandra Cisneros," *Major Authors and Illustrators for Children and Young Adults*, 2nd ed., 8 vols., Gale Group, 2002, reproduced in *Biography Resource Center* (Farmington Hills, Mich.: Thomson Gale, 2007), <http://www.edupaperback.org/showauth.cfm?authid=259> (October 25, 2007).

14. "Corrections and Citations," *Chicago Tribune*, October 28, 1998, p. 3.

15. Ibid.

16. Sandra Cisneros, "Alfredo Cisneros Del Moral Foundation," *SandraCisneros.com*, n.d., <http://www.sandracisneros.com/foundation.php> (August 1, 2008).

17. Cassandra West, "Multimedia Listener's Guide," *Chicago Tribune*, September 13, 1998, Book Section, p. 8.

18. Maria Newman, "Sandra Cisneros: Her New Book, Her New Look," *Hispanic Online*, September 2002, <http://www.hispaniconline.com/magazine/2002/sep/CoverStory/index.html> (August 13, 2007).

CHAPTER 12. WRITING ALL ALONE IN HER PAJAMAS

1. Robert Birnbaum, "Sandra Cisneros: Author of *Caramelo* Talks With Robert Birnbaum," *Identity Theory*, December 4, 2002.

2. Jen Buckendorff, "Father's Death Opened New Insights for 'Caramelo' Author Sandra Cisneros," *Seattle Times*, October 21, 2003.

3. Maria Newman, "Sandra Cisneros: Her New Book, Her New Look," *Hispanic Online*, September 2002, <http://www.hispaniconline.com/magazine/2002/sep/CoverStory/index.html> (August 13, 2007)

4. Margaret Randall, "Weaving a Spell," *Women's Review of Books*, October 1, 2002.

5. Diane Urbani, "Cisneros Takes Adoring Audience for Ride," *Deseret Morning News*, September 21, 2003, *FindArticles.com*, October 15, 2008, <http://findarticles.com/p/articles/mi_qn4188/is_20030921/ai_n11416161> (October 15, 2008).

6. Randall.

7. Ana Caban, "'Mango Street' Ripens Into Lyrical Literary Success," *Milwaukee Journal-Sentinel*, October 12, 2003, <http://www.jsonline.com/story/index.aspx?id=176182> (August 3, 2007).

8. Gayle Elliott, "An Interview With Sandra Cisneros," *Missouri Review*, Vol. 25, No. 1, Spring 2002, <http://moreview.com/content/dynamic/view_text.php?text_id=1093> (August 17, 2007).

9. "Sandra Cisneros Quotes," *Brainy Quotes*, 2008, <http://www.brainyquote.com/quotes/authors/s/ sandra_cisneros.html> (August 15, 2007).

10. Buckendorff.

11. Ibid.

12. Ibid.

13. Elliott.

14. Sandra Cisneros, "Border Crossings and Beyond," *Studies in Short Fiction*, Summer 1994, Vol. 31, No. 3, p. 415, Literature of the American Minorities class Web site, Edgwood College Department of English, April 25, 2000,

<http://english.edgewood.edu/eng242/Sandra_Cisneros_Border_Crossings_and_beyond.htm> (August 17, 2007).

15. Jim Sagel, "Sandra Cisneros: Conveying the Riches of the Latin American Culture Is the Author's Literary Goal," *Publisher's Weekly*, March 29, 1991, *Las Mujeres*, 2007, <http://www.lasmujeres.com/en/?m=sandra-cisneros&s=articles&sc=art_conveying-the-riches> (August 15, 2007).

16. "Sandra Cisneros," *Major Authors and Illustrators for Children and Young Adults*, 2nd ed., 8 vols., Gale Group, 2002, reproduced in *Biography Resource Center* (Farmington Hills, Mich.: Thomson Gale, 2007), <http://www.edupaperback.org/showauth.cfm?authid=259> (October 25, 2007).

17. Urbani.

18. Sandra Cisneros, "Macondo Foundation's Elvira Cordero Cisneros Award 2008," *Macondo Foundation, Inc.*, n.d., <http://www.macondofoundation.org/programs_elvira.html> (August 1, 2008).

19. Elaine Ayala, "Macondo Libre Readies for Liberating Words," *Latino Life*, June 5, 2008, <http://blogs.mysanantonio.com/weblogs/latinlife/2008/06/macondo_libre_readies_for_libe.html> (October 15, 2008).

Books by Sandra Cisneros

1980 *Bad Boys*

1984 *The House on Mango Street*

1987 *My Wicked Wicked Ways*

1991 *Woman Hollering Creek and Other Stories*

1994 *Hairs/Pelitos*

Loose Woman

La Casa en Mango Street (Spanish version)

2002 *Caramelo*

2004 *Vintage Cisneros*

Glossary

advance—Money paid to an author for a book that is still to be completed.

Anglo—Spanish word that refers to white people.

barrio—Spanish word for "neighborhood." In the United States, the word is used to describe city neighborhoods where Latinos primarily live.

bungalow—Small, one-story house.

card catalog—Filing system used to organize library books before there were computers.

chicana (female)/chicano (male)—Refers to people of Mexican heritage born in the United States, who developed a political consciousness during the civil-rights movement.

class—Different groups within a culture or society, often determined by economic status.

commission—Group authorized to perform certain duties.

Communist—Governed by a system in which all property and goods are owned by the community at large and is used to benefit all citizens; a central government describes how to distribute everything.

context—Part of a text or statement that surrounds a particular word or passage and determines its meaning.

controversy—Dispute.

crannies—Small, narrow openings in a wall.

discrimination—Treatment of, or making a distinction in favor of or against, a person or thing based on the group, class, or category to which that person or thing belongs rather than on individual merit.

diversity—Variety.

doctorate—Degree given by a university following several years of additional study and research after a master's degree.

ecology—Study of the environment.

ethnic—Characteristic of a people, especially a group sharing a common and distinctive culture, religion, language, or the like.

fellowship—Money paid to support a student doing advance study in a field.

gender—Male or female.

green card—The popular term for a registration card granting a citizen of another country permission to live and work in the United States.

Hispanic—Relating to a Spanish-speaking people or culture.

indigenous people—Ethnic group who inhabit the geographic region with which they have the earliest historical connection.

intuition—Ability to know things without conscious reasoning.

Latina (female)/Latino (male)—People from various Central and Latin American or Spanish-speaking Caribbean countries who have immigrated to the United States.

mainstream literature—Books that a wide variety of the population chooses to read.

master's degree—Degree given by college to a person who has completed a prescribed course of study after earning a bachelor's degree.

metaphor—Figure of speech containing an implied comparison.

migrant worker—Person who moves from place to place to get work, especially a farm laborer who harvests crops seasonally.

people of color—People of different races.

poignant—Emotionally touching or moving.

racism—Belief among the various human races involving the idea that one's own race is superior and has the right to rule others.

recruiter—Person who tries to enroll students at a school or college, often with an offer of grants or scholarships.

segregation—Separation of people due to bias or prejudice against a particular group.

sexism—Discrimination based on gender, especially discrimination against women.

stereotype—Generalization, usually exaggerated or oversimplified and often offensive, that is used to describe or distinguish a group.

tenement—Apartment building usually in a poor neighborhood.

undocumented immigrant—Someone not born in the United States who enters the country without legal permission.

Further Reading

BOOKS

Carlson, Lori M. *Cool Salsa: Bilingual Poems on Growing Up Latino in the United States*. New York: H. Holt and Company, 2008.

Carlson, Lori M., Flavio Marais, and Manuel River-Ortez. *Voices in First Person: Reflections on Latino Identity*. New York: Atheneum, 2008.

Chong, Nilda, and Francia Baez. *Latino Culture: A Dynamic Force in the Changing American Workplace*. Boston: International Press, 2005

Windows Into My World: Latino Youth Write Their Lives. Houston, Tex.: Piñata Books, 2007.

INTERNET ADDRESSES

Macondo Foundation, Inc.
http://www.macondoworkshop.org

Planet Tolerance
http://www.tolerance.org/pt/index.html

Sandra Cisneros
http://www.sandracisneros.com

Index